YEADON'S REGISTER

of

L N E R

LOCOMOTIVES

Volume Ten

GRESLEY D49 & J38 CLASSES

ISBN 1 899624 12 0

DEDICATION

To Annie and Jean, also to those who from 1932 to 1957, relied on D49s to get them to school, college, factory, office, family re-unions, and to seaside holidays: also to the photographers who provided such a wealth of material for my research, and for your memories.

First published in the United Kingdom by
CHALLENGER PUBLICATIONS
15 Lovers Lane, Grasscroft, Oldham, OL4 4DP
Printed and bound by Amadeus Press, Huddersfield

INTRODUCTION

You are well entitled to ask why such diverse classes as D49 and J38 should be paired to form Volume 10, especially when class J39 had even more in common with class D49. There are two valid reasons for that choice - one provided by the LNER, and the other by my publisher. Taking the latter first; there were 289 engines to deal with in class J39, so they need their own book which (hopefully) will follow as Volume 11, and 35 class J38 sit more comfortably with 76 class D49 from a production aspect. The LNER connection is that, despite D49 being for express passenger work (albeit in the secondary range) and J38 being mainly for coal haulage, their steam raising facility was common to both classes; indeed, some D49 boilers found further use on class J38 in their later years, and some tenders served with both classes.

All 35 of the 0-6-0 type worked the whole of their average 40 years life in the Scottish Area, so apart from at Carlisle, sightings south of the border were rare, and such as did occur arose almost entirely from a change of tender type in the early 1930's for which some visited Darlington works. The original order for the D49 class - those which came to be known as the "Shires" - was comprised of 15 carrying the names of Scottish counties, all allocated to work in the Scottish Area, and 13 with English county names for North Eastern Area. The class was later augmented by 48, and because 40 of them did almost all their work in the area bounded by Newcastle, Hull, and Leeds, one tends to overlook the substantial amount of work the D49 class did in Scotland throughout its thirty years existence. At sheds such as Dundee, Thornton, and Edinburgh St Margarets both classes were looked on as equally important.

D49 CLASS DEVELOPMENT

The original order for this class was placed with Darlington works on 16th April 1926, and was only for engines, because it clearly specified that the tenders would be built by Doncaster works. The 28 engines were to be of three significantly different designs; the first 20 had piston valves driven by Walschaerts gear, and their diagram showed Part 1. The next six had Lentz poppet valves and oscillating cams also driven by Walschaerts gear, and their diagram had Part 3 on it, whilst the final two continued to be referred to as "compounds" until well into 1927, but when they did make their final appearance in 1929 they had Lentz poppet valves but rotary cam operated, and they were the Part 2. Further building added eight to Part 1 and no less than forty to Part 2, but the six in Part 3 were all rebuilt in 1938 with piston instead of poppet valves, which added six to Part 1 but eliminated Part 3.

The nameplates of the first twenty-eight all included 'shire' ending, as did five of the eight added in 1929, the remaining three being NORTHUMBERLAND, CUMBERLAND, and WESTMORLAND. A curiosity of the naming was that county Durham was totally ignored despite all being built there. When it was decided in 1932 that further building would be to Part 2, names of Hunts were chosen for them, so the existing pair 352 LEICESTERSHIRE and 336 BUCKINGHAMSHIRE were re-named to those of Hunts.

The first twenty went into traffic displaying their number by 12" shaded transfers on the tender, and certainly so did the first five of the six Part 3 engines. The last of that batch 335

First of class no. 234 did not enter traffic until 29th October, but here on Tuesday 27th September 1927, Darlington had hurriedly pushed it to completion for inspection by the Directors on the Locomotive Committee. Painted only in undercoat (not works grey) it is lacking both lining and nameplates. Note on the side of the smokebox there is an outlet for a pyrometer connection, but only 234 was so fitted. *WBY collection*

Six out of the first batch built, in which was 249 ABERDEENSHIRE, were fitted with Woodall connection rods. That type had their outside big end forked to take the front end of the coupling rod between the jaws. The others had, and kept, normal type rods. *Photomatic*

BEDFORDSHIRE left Darlington on 28th August 1928, which was before that works made the change of number position from tender to cab side as standard practice. So 335 presumably first had its number on the tender, although no photographic proof of that has ever been seen. Doubt arises from one of the illustrations that I have included, and which shows number on the cab *before* 335 was changed from vertical lever for driving the middle valve gear. For that alteration it went into Darlington on 15th March 1930, but it had been in the works from 28th January to 25th February 1929 for a non-classified repair, at which the number position *may* have been changed. All those added to the class starting with 2753 CHESHIRE in February 1929 had their number on the cab from new, and that also applied to 352 and 336 when they appeared in March and June 1929.

During the 1939-45 war all 76 lost their lined green paint, and it was never restored to them. They also had L N E R reduced to only N E, but they did recover the full initials before nationalisation, and British Railways did accord them full lining on black paint. In 1941/42 when they were deprived of Group Standard tender, mainly at their shed, it was not unusual to see some cases of a green painted engine coupled with an unlined black tender.

The six Part 3 engines originally had vertical levers to operate the middle valve gear, but that arrangement turned out to be troublesome, so from June 1929 to September 1930, they were altered to use Gresley's 2 to 1 horizontal lever instead. With the vertical levers there was a small box cover on the running plate, but modellers need to note that disappeared when the gear was changed.

The 15 Part 2 engines built in 1932/33 were fitted with Goodall articulated drawbar between engine and tender. However,

that speciality inhibited exchanging of tenders, and was also a handicap to less skilled maintenance during the war. On 7th April 1941 Gresley agreed that they be changed to the standard solid drawbar when they next went through the works for repair. It is very likely that would be his last design decision because exactly four weeks later he was dead. That change began in November 1941, and was completed in June 1944, but it is not discernible in photographs.

Only on the last five of Part 2 was a train heater connection at the front fitted when new, but many subsequently acquired that facility. Its hose below the buffer beam should not be confused with a brake pipe connection. The first 28 engines were all to work in N.E. and Scottish Areas so were equipped with Westinghouse air brake, because they were built before the *Unification of Brakes Programme* became effective in 1929. For that brake, Darlington fitted the front end connection below the buffer beam, but it had been removed, along with the pump, before the train heater connection began to be put on there.

THE THOMPSON ALTERATION TO 365 "THE MORPETH"

Conversion of this engine from 3-cylinder poppet valve to 2-cylinder piston valve was not a success. Presumably it even disappointed Thompson, because he strongly discouraged all attempts by the railway press to give any publicity to it. Anyone sufficiently interested is referred to the full account which the Railway Correspondence & Travel Society were able to include in Part 4 of their *Locomotives of the L N E R* series.

Suffice it here to register its classification. When it went to traffic in August 1942 the Running Supt's Weekly Transfers showed it as re-classified to D49/4, and Darlington had put that on its front buffer beam. On 10th December 1942 a brief note simply initialled "E.T." instructed the Chief Draughtsman at Doncaster that it should be classified "D". That was how it was titled on its diagram issued with 1942 yearly alterations, but Weekly Transfers continued to use D49/4, which was also still to be seen on the buffer beam even after it was renumbered by British Railways to 62768 in August 1948.

OTHER CHANGES OF DETAIL - MAJOR AND MINOR

There was a plethora of them, some applicable to only a single engine (such as the M.L.S. superheater and multiple valve regulator on 335) whilst others were widely spread, for example, Raven fog signalling apparatus on N.E. Area engines, and - later Hudd Automatic Train Control equipment in Scottish Area. To the discerning eye, many small differences and changes could be noted. The first twenty were fitted with North Eastern design steam reversing gear, regarded with distaste by the drivers of the fourteen Part 1s sent to work in Scottish Area. Even as early as March 1929 Cowlairs works began to change them to screw reverse, and on the first three (nos.270, 250 and 264) they used a straight operating rod. For the other eleven, starting in June, they worked to a Darlington drawing, on which the rod had a downward curve at both ends and a lower exit from the cab front. So on the first three the rod was *above* the nameplate, but behind it on the others. The six engines in N.E. Area were also changed from steam to screw reverse (with Darlington style rod) but not until April 1935 to January 1937.

The drawings for the first batch built revealed that, by mistake, provision of footsteps for access to the front end had not been included. Nos.307, 309, 310 and 311 were so fitted when new, but the previous sixteen had left works before remedial action was taken. Suitable material was soon sent to their sheds for steps to be added.

In that initial batch, just the first six were fitted with Woodard connecting rods on which the outside big end was forked so that the front end of the coupling rod then fitted between the jaws. That United States patent proved sufficiently acceptable for thirty of the Hunt Part 2 engines to be similarly equipped.

Smokebox doors, cab side screens, mechanical lubricator arrangement, provision for tablet catching apparatus, clips for carrying NBR type destination boards, and altered balancing in the coupled wheels, were all items having discernible variation between individual engines. The best help I can give modellers on them is to describe those differences in the captions to appropriate illustrations that I have been able to include.

TENDERS

All 76 D49s were first coupled with the Group Standard 7½ tons coal and 4200 gallons water type which had water pick up apparatus fitted. The latter provision had not been thought through properly when fifteen of the first batch were to work in Scottish Area, because there were no track troughs in that Area. The twenty-eight which Doncaster built were to the original design which had sides with stepped out top, and they were put with the 'Shires' with numbers up to, and including, 352. The additional eight Part 1 engines built in 1929 and numbered 2753 to 2760 received tenders of the same capacities built by Darlington but of the later flush sided type.

When the order for fifteen of the Hunt variety was placed with Darlington on 5th December 1929 it was for engines and tenders, the engines to be numbered in the 201 to 298 range. Fifteen flush sided tenders were duly completed, but on 18th December 1930 the order was amended to the smaller 3500 gallons type and lacked water pick up apparatus, the intention being to use them in Scottish Area on J38 class - for which they were entirely adequate - and so cascade their larger tenders with pick up gear to be coupled with the D49 Part 2 engines on that order. So, beginning with J38 class 1422 in October 1931, eight J38s were called to Darlington works for exchange of tender, and the opportunity was taken of also giving them a general repair. The other seven new tenders were ferried to Scotland for the change to be made at sheds or by Cowlairs works. The fifteen

On 23rd December 1937 Darlington turned out no.214 THE ATHERSTONE which had been painted specially with "Syntholux" to see if its cost could be justified by durability. So far as is known, it remained a "one-off" and the condition of 258 shows that there was little, if any, improvement in appearance compared with normal painting. *LNER*

264 STIRLINGSHIRE on the turntable at Eastfield shed in Glasgow, shows that, by a mistake, no footsteps were fitted at the front end, although they were soon added. All the first 28 were dual fitted for braking, Westinghouse air braked coaches then being still extensively used by both North Eastern, and by Scottish Areas, where these engines were to work. Note its compressor ahead of the cab, and the train connecting hose under the buffer beam. The whole class always had Group Standard buffers, but only the first 20 in Part 1 had circular cover around the base of the safety valves. *J.J.Cunningham*

stepped top 4200 gallons tenders released from the J38 class were then spruced up, changed from black to green painting, and duly coupled to the Hunts number 201 to 298. Those fifteen were the ones with Goodall articulated drawbar between engine and tender.

The further order for 25 Hunts placed on 1st November 1933 had no complications regarding tenders, and Darlington built Group Standard flush sided 4200 gallons type for all of them. Until 1938, all 76 had tender of the same high capacity, 43 with stepped top and 33 flush sided. All could pick up water from track troughs, but their duties rarely required them to do so. Only very occasionally did those on the Leeds-Newcastle expresses have that need, and it was realised that again there was an opportunity to use existing tenders to better purpose. The 1938 rebuilding of five Part 3 engines to Part 1 was accompanied by coupling them with ex NER self-trimming tenders from Q6 class mineral engines, carrying $5\frac{1}{2}$ tons coal and 4125 gallons water, but not fitted with scoop. A similar change was made on 256 of Part 1 and on 336 of Part 2, which together released seven Group Standard tenders to serve new V2 class engines which Darlington then had under construction. The replacement tenders for the Q6 class which had been denuded came from life expired mixed traffic engines on the withdrawal list.

War demands for steel carried that tender changing process even further, because in 1941/42 all the other piston valve engines of class D49 lost their Group Standard 4200 gallons tender, twenty stepped top, and eight flush sided ones being sent to Doncaster for that works to couple twenty-five of them with class O2 engines they were building, the surplus three replacing 3500 gallons GNR type to provide enhanced capacity for three class K3 engines. On those twenty-eight D49 class the replacements were ex Great Central 4000 gallons type no longer required by 0-8-0 goods engines, and because their sides had stepped top, overall appearance seemed little changed. Fortunately, tender type with a D49 was easily established from the frame slots; on Group Standard top and bottom were parallel and the front one was

noticeably longer than the rear one. On the ex Great Central tenders, the slots were of equal length, and the top was appreciably curved.

Apart from 336 getting NER tender in 1938, the Part 2 Hunt class were immune from tender alterations, and generally remained so. Incidentally, the other original Part 2 no.352 was the only one to retain a tender which Doncaster had built against the 1926 order. That tender was also singular in being doubly numbered, and plated accordingly, with one in the Doncaster 5xxx series and also one in the Darlington 7xxx series introduced in March 1938.

In February 1947, to facilitate exchange of tenders at repairs, a spare Q6 type tender was coupled with 2756, and in April 1949 a similar tender left works with 62752. At that date, some of the Great Central type tenders were being rebuilt with flush sides, so the extra tender was introduced to avoid delay in turning out engines from repairs. In November 1955 an NER tender was coupled with 62739, replaced in May 1958 by a GC flush sided rebuild, which it then kept to October 1960 withdrawal. Only one other GC type went to a Hunt; on 24th October 1958 an example with a stepped top was put with 62741 simply to go with it for withdrawal, and 62741's Group Standard type then served exactly another year with 62722 of Part 1.

D49 CLASS REGISTRATION

With my home being in Hull where, at one time or another, no fewer than 34 of the 76 class D49 were shedded, and 26 others regularly working in here from their York, and Leeds sheds, one rather took them for granted, certainly until the Thompson B1 class supplanted them after the 1939-45 war. The first D49 entry in my manuscript register is (very appropriately) 273 THE HOLDERNESS in York station on 6th April 1933 on the 8.55 a.m. Leeds to Glasgow express in which it took me as far as Newcastle. That was the train ultimately named 'The North

Part 1 of the class was given to the initial twenty, which had numbers between 234 and 311. They had piston valves operated by Walschaerts gear, and their reversing gear was steam operated. No.277 BERWICKSHIRE here at Carlisle in 1928 was one of the fourteen in the first batch with normal connecting rods, and front footsteps have already been added. *J.J.Cunningham*

Briton', and on which the same staff could serve you with Breakfast, Morning Coffee, Luncheon, Afternoon Tea, and Dinner. Curiously, the next one built after 273 (and only twelve days later) was to elude my registration until it was the last of the D49 class to be noted. It was 16th September 1944 before I logged 282 THE HURWORTH, which was then taking the 10.45 a.m. out of Carlisle to Newcastle, and it was all the more frustrating because it had been shedded in Hull from May 1933 to June 1939, but that was before I began systematic recording of LNER locomotives. That Hurworth name turned up again to haunt me of missed opportunities more than fifty years later. Our nephew was then commanding officer of the Royal Navy mine hunter of that name, and had invited my wife and I to Rosyth to inspect his ship. We had booked an hotel in Edinburgh when Saddam Hussain started causing trouble and H.M.S. Hurworth was hurriedly despatched to take up station in the Gulf. So we had to settle for a photograph of it passing under the Forth Bridge, because when it did return, promotion had moved our nephew to another ship.

The extensive rebuilding of 365 THE MORPETH needed a double entry. In original form I saw it on 16th August 1936 in Hull (Paragon) with a train from Leeds, and in its emasculated Thompson version, I was in Leeds City South station on 5th June 1943 when it brought in the 10.45 a.m. slow passenger train from York. On Good Friday 30th March 1945 it actually hauled me (and family) on the 4.30 p.m. from Leeds to Scarborough.

Not until the beginning of January 1940 did I begin to record *all* the LNER locos hauling trains in which I travelled, and the first entry is on the 13th when Hull shedded D49 234 YORKSHIRE took me on the 1.00 p.m. from Hull to Leeds. That same engine, by then numbered 62700 also brought me from Leeds to Hull on 31st October 1957 in the 5.07 p.m. departure.

On the following day I had my last haulage behind one of the Hunt variety, 62754 THE BERKELEY being on the 4.00 p.m. from Doncaster to Hull. By then D49 class was on the withdrawal list, and my final trip behind one had 62701 DERBYSHIRE taking me in the 9.12 a.m. from Hull to Doncaster on 29th January 1958.

The D49s shedded at Hull Botanic Gardens worked to Scarborough, Leeds, Doncaster, York, and to both Victoria and Midland stations in Sheffield, on all of which lines I was able to travel behind them. Bridlington shed had two of this class for working its residential business trains, one to and from Hull, and the other via Driffield and Selby to Leeds. The portion of that route between Driffield and Selby was outside my normal scope for haulage by a D49, but on 24th July 1949 returning to Hull on the 8.00 p.m. from Leeds, 62720 WARWICKSHIRE took the Selby to Market Weighton line, and then diverged to reach Hull via Beverley.

Those allocated to Leeds Neville Hill shed specialised on working their trains to and from Newcastle via York and Darlington, and also via Harrogate, Stockton and the coast line. I was frequently hauled by a D49 on both routes, one of them still conjuring up vivid memories. On Tuesday 29th April 1942 travelling to Leeds, I joined the 5.22 p.m. at Darlington which, as usual, was worked by two Neville Hill D49 class, on that occasion 357 THE FERNIE leading 375 THE SOUTH DURHAM. We left punctually, but until reaching Thirsk, we drew to a crawl at each main line signal box for a verbal message to be shouted to the drivers. I was also puzzled by the total absence of any traffic passing us on the opposite track, so I suspected there had been an accident further south resulting in our being diverted at some junction. After Thirsk we ran at normal speed, and the cause

The twenty Part 1 engines were followed by a batch of six designated Part 3. They had poppet instead of piston valves, and oscillating cams to operate them. As built, vertical levers from the Walschaerts gear worked that to the cams, and at the top of each lever was a small box cover, mounted on the running plate. They also differed from Part 1 by not having a base cover to their safety valves. 329 was the last new D49 to have its number displayed on the tender. *WBY collection*

of that strange progress became only too obvious when we took the big left-hand curve to run alongside York Clifton locomotive yard. The large school which overlooked the line from the Poppleton Road side had a great V-shaped gap instead of its centre portion, and we then passed a couple of cranes attempting to lift a damaged coach, which simply disintegrated before our eyes from the effect of blast damage. Next was the shock of seeing York North shed torn wide open, and the incredible sight of A4 no.4469, and B16 no.925 lying mortally wounded. It was all the more unreal to me because, on that and the two previous days, I had been engaged full time on special work in the Royal Ordnance Factory at Birtley, without access to newspapers or to radio news. So I was completely unaware of the air raid on York in the early hours of that morning, and when we stopped at the main up platform in the station, we learned that we were the first train allowed into the station since the raid. The burnt-out coaches of the London-Edinburgh express were still in the main down platform line, but I can clearly recall the crunching of glass on the track by the pair of Hunts as they gingerly drew to a halt, before going on to Leeds.

York's allocation of D49 class worked to Scarborough, Leeds, both Sheffield stations and as far as Lincoln on the Continental boat trains. I traversed all those lines, but only on the Scarborough and Leeds journeys was I lucky enough to be hauled by D49 class. Further north my D49 runs were much more patchy, although they did include Carlisle to Newcastle, and the Waverley route into Edinburgh; also from there to Perth behind 250 PERTHSHIRE. I also had 2706 FORFARSHIRE on the 9.59 a.m. Leuchars Junction to Kirkcaldy, so although not complete, I did have wide-ranging knowledge of how, and where, D49 class operated.

It will have been noted that any sighting of a D49 south of Sheffield or Lincoln merits special mention, and I would be more than happy to be told of any factual observations subsequent to 1929. When 234 YORKSHIRE was new in November 1927, York shed loaned it to the GC Section for three weeks, and during them, it worked into and out of London's Marylebone station. Then, from 29th September 1928 until 29th April 1929 booster-fitted ex GN Atlantic 4419 worked in North Eastern Area from Leeds Neville Hill shed, and they sent their 245 LINCOLNSHIRE to King's Cross shed as balancing stock. I did not observe either of those interesting workings by D49 class because my serious study of LNER locomotives had not then begun. There was certainly one visit to London by 256, on a football Cup Final excursion, as shown by a photograph of it at Top Shed. A solitary Hunt no.283 THE MIDDLETON, although shedded at Leeds Neville Hill, was reported to have reached Peterborough during June 1942.

In total, I experienced haulage by fifty-two out of the seventy-six in the class, and of the twenty-four that I missed, eleven worked the whole of their lives in Scottish Area. Three others did work for an average of about five years from Hull Botanic Gardens shed in the later 1930's, but I did not put on paper every haulage by an LNER loco until the beginning of 1940. I do have notes of seeing all three (including the elusive HURWORTH) in Paragon station during 1933-35 when it was probable that I was making a journey from there, but haulage is "not proven". Two of the others not to haul me also came to be shedded in Hull, but not until 13th September 1959, and by then it was even rare for a D49 to be seen in use. That pair were at Dairycoates shed, in store, until they both went for withdrawal and cutting up on 16th January 1961.

RE-NUMBERING

Those not old enough to have seen D49 class in their original numbering need to be made aware of possible confusion. When the whole of the LNER locomotive stock underwent renumbering in 1946, the 76 D49 class were allocated new numbers 2700 to 2775, mainly in the sequence of the date they entered traffic, but the eight Part 1 built in 1929 were carrying 2753 to 2760. Between 7th April to 1st December they were changed and became 2728 to 2735; that then enabled eight Hunts (nos.217, 222, 226, 230, 238, 258, 274 and 279) to take 2753 to 2760. CHESHIRE lost 2753 on 7th April, and THE BELVOIR became 2753 (instead of 217) on 28th April 1946. Fortunately for observers, if you saw any of 2753-60 with a normal nameplate it was a Part 1 Shire, but if it had a fox above the plate, it was a renumbered Part 2 Hunt.

PRESERVATION

For D49 class we do not just have to make do with memories, because when 62712 MORAYSHIRE was withdrawn from running stock on 3rd July 1961, as 'last of class' it became a stationary boiler supplying steam to Slateford Laundry. By the time that duty finished, a Scottish enthusiast Mr Ian Fraser, was able in July 1964 to buy it for restoration to running condition, which Inverurie works completed on 5th January 1965. It is now in the care of the Scottish Railway Preservation Society, and can be seen near Falkirk.

J38 CLASS SCOTTISH AREA GOODS ENGINES

After the Grouping, which founded the LNER on 1st January 1923, additions to its locomotive stock continued to be to designs from its component Companies through 1923 and 1924. In 1925 the single Garratt banking engine did appear, but its engine portion was largely just a pair of Great Northern 2-8-0 type of O2 class. Almost simultaneously the P1 class was introduced, but that was simply the Great Northern Pacific boiler on an altered wheel arrangement.

The first evidence of a Group design is dated 4th March 1925, when Darlington works received order CME 101 to build 55 goods engines and tenders, 0-6-0 type, 20 for N.E.Area, and 35 for Scottish Area. That only indicated a different move to new ground, because design was to be "Class J27 Modified", and J27 was the LNER's classification of the North Eastern Railway's most modern 0-6-0, although the design dated from 1906, to which a superheater had been added from 1921. The order was then amended on 12th June 1925 by the cancellation of the 20 for N.E.Area, but the 35 for Scotland began to come out on 28th January 1926, and by 28th May 1926 the order had been completed. As those 17 weeks spanned the hiatus of the General Strike, when Darlington turned nothing out from 30th April until 17th May, there was certainly nothing wrong with the production rate at that works. Nor could anybody cavil at its quality, because the first of those 35 engines was not withdrawn until 29th December 1962, and 21 were still hard at work hauling coal trains into 1966, and the last one survived until April 1967.

The 'modification' to J27 design was applied almost totally, common features being limited to boiler diameter and pressure, the style of the smokebox door, and the commodious double window cab, despite J38 being a product of Darlington draughtsmen. So J38 without doubt could claim to be the first LNER locomotive design, and one that never needed extensive, or expensive, alterations throughout its forty years of earning considerable revenue. Certainly there were changes of detail, and descriptions of them can be found in the captions to the illustrations showing them.

When the LNER introduced boiler diagram numbers in 1928, the 35 boilers which Darlington had built for this class were given 97A, and there were no subsequent additions. By

This is Darlington's official record, showing the first of the class as built, but in works grey painting. Details to note are the small diameter pipe from the cab to the steam reversing gear, the steam for the whistle taken from the manifold inside the cab, the circular cover around the base of the safety valves, the double-case buffers at the front, and a smokebox length of 4' 2³/₄", all items to which subsequent change was made. The original coupling of a 4200 gallons Group Standard tender is also clearly shown; all 35 lost that tender type during 1931 to 1933. *LNER*

Between October 1931 and December 1933 all were changed to the 3500 gallons Group Standard flush sided tender, this Darlington photograph showing 1422 as it left that works on 1st December 1931. All these tenders had Group Standard buffer type. *LNER*

then, a design 6" shorter between the tubeplates (but with the same length of barrel) had been adopted as standard both for J39 and D49 classes, and well over 100 were already at work, so that type took precedence as Diagram 97. In 1932 one of them was used for providing a spare to permit interchanging on J38 class, engine 1406 being the recipient, and in 1935, three more Diagram 97 boilers went to J38 class. There was certainly nothing wrong with Diagram 97A boilers, because the youngest served 16 years, and the last two only ceased work in December 1962 and November 1963 respectively.

DETAIL CHANGES DISCERNIBLE ON J38 CLASS

Until December 1932, when a newly built boiler of Diagram 97 was introduced to J38 class and fitted to 1406, all carried the 97A boiler, and when those of that type reached the end of their economic life, Diagram 97 was used in replacement. The type in use could be identified, because on Diagram 97 the chimney and anti-vacuum valve were set 6" further back than on 97A boilers.

As mentioned in D49 class, until October 1931 all had 4200 gallons Group Standard tender with sides stepped out at the top, and although not needed, had water pick up apparatus. By December 1933 all thirty-five had been changed to the 3500 gallons Group Standard flush sided type, which was not fitted for replenishing from track troughs. Twelve of those replacements were built by Doncaster, with the other twenty-three made at Darlington works. In later British Railways days two other tender types were seen with J38 class, one probably due to mistaken identity for a J39 by Cowlairs works, which resulted in 65916 from 19th September to 24th October 1953, and 65902 from 27th August to 1st October 1955 being coupled with North Eastern 4125 gallons coal rail type. The two tenders concerned were not without some distinction because they had been built for, and ran for some years with A2 class Pacifics 2402 CITY OF YORK and 2400 CITY OF NEWCASTLE respectively. Both engines were quickly restored to Doncaster built 3500 gallons type. Then, released from withdrawn members of the K3 class, 65904 on 14th February 1959, and 65919 on 16th September 1961 reverted to the 4200 gallons Group Standard type (although flush sided) and both then kept them until their July and August 1964 withdrawal.

From new, J38 had steam operated reversing gear as standard, and contrasting with that gear's Scottish experience on D49 class, it was used satisfactorily for almost twenty years. Beginning with 1403 in February 1945, change to screw operated began, and by June 1948, all had been so altered.

Small detail changes of lesser significance concerned front end coupling and brake connecting pipe, top lamp iron type and its position, smokebox door fastening, steam supply to the whistle, cover at base of safety valves, drop grate operating gear, type of front buffers, a wide variety of paintings, lettering and numbering, and finally some of them acquiring BR Automatic Warning System. All these have been given attention in the captions to the illustrations to assist modellers to achieve accurate representation.

REGISTRATION OF J38 CLASS

My first opportunity for recording this class was on 17th July 1937 when I examined 1416 at St Margarets shed in Edinburgh. By 11th August 1946 I had seen all except two in their original numbering, and that day at Dunfermline shed I noted 1446 with its new 5933 numbering. That left only 1403 to complete the class, and it was not until 20th August 1949 when I made contact with it at Ferryhill shed in Aberdeen. By then its number was 5902, but the tender still carried L N E R, to my personal satisfaction.

Designed for goods traffic, this class was equipped with steam brake on engine and tender, but it was also fitted with vacuum ejector, and piped for train braking, which allowed it to be used on coaching stock. In the 1930's, instead of coal from Fife coalfield, some were used on holiday Saturdays for passenger trains to and from Fife coast resorts. There were also occasions when their power came in handy hauling heavy trains crammed with football supporters. They could also be seen sometimes on station pilot duties, but I was never able to organise to be in a train hauled by one of this class. Normally to be seen on the main line, from Carlisle to Edinburgh, Dundee and Aberdeen, I did note some off that well beaten track, examples being 1422 at Gateshead shed on 16th April 1940, 1420 on a down Peebles branch goods at Leadburn on 14th July 1941, and 1442 on 25th July 1944 with the pick-up goods at Jedburgh station.

This is Doncaster's official record of the twelve tenders which they built for that change, and as they were ferried to Scotland for sheds to make the exchange, there was a temporary fitting of buffers and 3-link coupling at their front end. Doncaster had also applied red lining on the paint, but from 1929 the engines became unlined, so for a short period there were plain engines with lined tenders to be seen. *LNER*

The 35 boilers built for the class in 1926 proved very durable, and some survived in service until 1963. Here at Dunfermline shed in August 1957 is 1443's original boiler which 65928 carried from June 1957 to its withdrawal on 29th December 1962. *J.L.Stevenson*

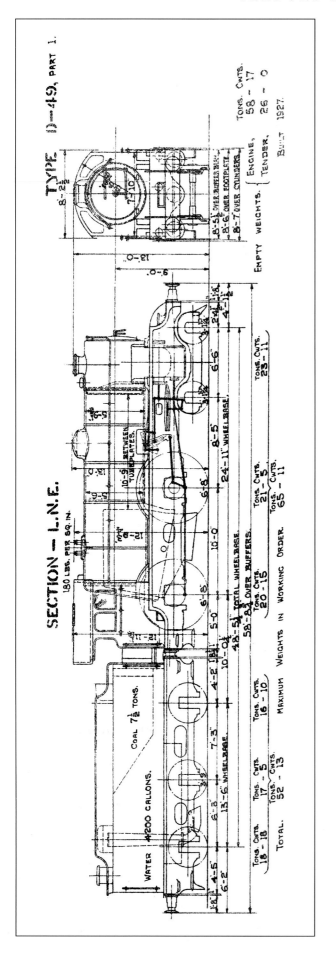

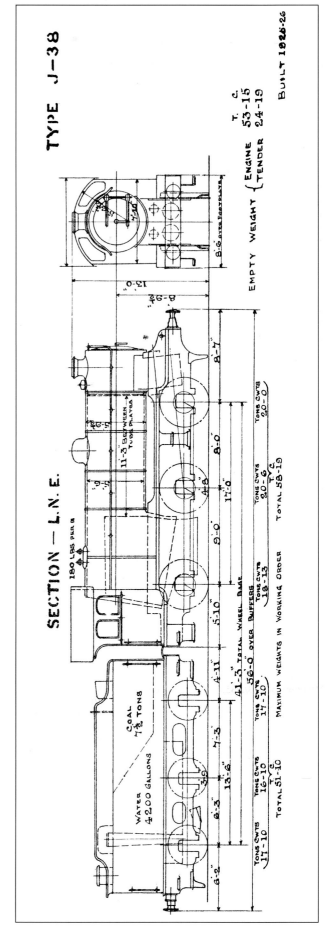

D49 CLASS

234 YORKSHIRE

Darlington.

To traffic 29/10/27.

REPAIRS:
Dar. 7-31/5/28.**L.**
Dar. 13/8-6/9/29.**L.**
Dar. 3/3-9/5/30.**G.**
Dar. 26/9-10/10/30.**N/C.**
Dar. 29/7-10/8/31.**N/C.**
Dar. 24/2-23/3/32.*Tender.*
Dar. 30/3-23/5/32.**G.**
Dar. 18/8-29/9/33.**G.**
Dar. 24/12/34-23/2/35.**G.**
Dar. 3/6-1/8/36.**G.**
Dar. 15/3-8/4/37.**L.**
Dar. 1/3-14/5/38.**G.** *Heat.conn.at front.*
Dar. 4/4-3/5/40.**G.**
Dar. 8/1-10/2/42.**G.**
Dar. 29/9-2/10/43.**N/C.**
Cow. 31/1-18/3/44.**G.**
Cow. 31/5-7/6/44.*Tender.*
Cow. 23/9-4/11/44.**L.**
Cow. 1-8/9/45.**L.**
Cow. 10/11/45-12/1/46.**G.**
Ghd. 31/11-31/12/47.**L.**
Dar. 4/12/48-1/4/49.**G.**
Dar. 4-8/4/49.**N/C.**
Dar. 22/5-14/6/50.**C/L.**
Dar. 3/5-2/6/51.**G.**
Dar. 7-16/6/51.**N/C.**
Dar. 8/5-13/6/53.**H/I.**
Dar. 15-16/6/53.**N/C.**
Dar. 2-16/9/53.**C/L.**
Dar. 19/4-20/5/55.**G.**
Dar. 4-22/6/56.**C/L.**
Dar. 22/2-2/4/57.**G.**
Dar. 19/12/57-28/1/58.**C/L.** *After derailment.*

BOILERS:
1983.
2164 *(ex2753)* 29/9/33.
2154 *(ex2757)* 23/2/35.
2627 *(ex374)* 1/8/36.
2154 *(ex327)* 3/5/40.
2124 *(ex318)* 10/2/42.
2332 *(ex246)* 18/3/44.
2913 *(ex1580)* 12/1/46.
2598 *(ex2715)* 1/4/49.
27369 *(ex2767)* 16/6/51.
27412 *(ex2762)* 20/5/55.
27387 *(ex2737)* 2/4/57.

SHEDS:
York.
Gorton 25/11/27.*On loan.*

Neville Hill 12/12/27.
Hull Botanic Gardens 8/6/39.
Bridlington 23/9/56.
Hull Botanic Gardens 22/9/57.

RENUMBERED:
2700 14/4/46.
62700 1/4/49.

CONDEMNED:
8/10/58.

251 DERBYSHIRE

Darlington.

To traffic 26/11/27.

REPAIRS:
Dar. 19/9-16/10/28.**L.**
Dar. 19/3-19/4/29.**N/C.**.*'Kylala' blastpipe fit.*
Dar. 1/4-24/6/30.**G.** *'Kylala' blastpipe removed.*
Dar. 18/3-11/5/32.**G.**
Dar. 30/11/33-26/1/34.**G.**
Dar. 14/10-10/12/35.**G.**
Dar. 3/1-19/2/36.**N/C.** *For trials by test dept.*
Dar. 14/7-16/10/36.**L.**
Dar. 30/9-25/11/37.**G.** *Heat.conn.at front.*
Dar. 27/7-25/8/38.**L.**
Dar. 5-31/10/38.**N/C.**
Dar. 10/5-6/7/39.**G.** *Recessed smokebox front.*
Dar. 22/2-20/3/40.**N/C.**
Dar. 25/5-21/11/40. *Tender.*
Dar. 31/10-29/11/41.**G.**
Dar. 9-29/6/42.**N/C.**
Cow. 8/7-19/8/44.**G.**
Dar. 22/4-14/6/47.**G.**
Ghd. 24/5-10/6/48.**L.**
Dar. 3/11-3/12/49.**G.**
Dar. 24/1-23/2/52.**G.**
Dar. 11/8-11/9/53.**H/I.**
Dar. 23/11-30/12/53.**C/L.**
Dar. 27/9-27/10/55.**G.**
Dar. 9/9-5/10/57.**G.**
Dar. 7-8/10/57.**N/C.**
Dar. 14-15/10/57.**N/C.**
1/2-14/6/59. *In store at Springhead.*

BOILERS:
1996.
2002 *(ex264)* 26/1/34.
7948 *(ex211)* 10/12/35.
7947 *(ex247)* 25/11/37.

2603 *(ex247)* 29/11/41.
3788 *(new)* 14/6/47.
2768 *(ex2713)* 3/12/49.
27396 *(ex2737)* 23/2/52.
27439 *(new)* 27/10/55.
27428 *(ex2738)* 5/10/57.

SHEDS:
Neville Hill.
Hull Botanic Gardens 17/7/39.
Neville Hill 31/1/42.
Hull Botanic Gardens 2/6/43.
Bridlington 7/8/49.
Hull Botanic Gardens 9/1/55.
Bridlington 29/5/55.
Hull Botanic Gardens 22/9/57.
Hull Dairycoates 14/6/59.

RENUMBERED:
2701 1/12/46.
62701 10/6/48.

CONDEMNED:
24/9/59.

253 OXFORDSHIRE

Darlington.

To traffic 30/11/27.

REPAIRS:
Dar. 7-22/6/28.**L.**
Dar. 30/12/29-24/2/30.**G.**
Dar. 5-22/1/31.*Tender.*
Dar. 9/10-7/12/31.**G.**
Dar. 26/4-16/6/32.**H.** *New cylinders.*
Dar. 24/4-7/6/33.**G.**
Dar. 15/11/33-29/3/34.**H.** *Main frame fractured.*
Dar. 22/1-2/3/35.**G.**
Dar. 13/9-20/12/35.**L.** *Tender, after collision.*
Dar. 4/2-21/3/36.**G.**
Dar. 4/11-24/12/36.**G.**
Dar. 26/2-2/3/37.**N/C.**
Dar. 5/8-11/10/37.**G.** *New frames.*
Dar. 4/1-23/2/38.**H.** *New crank axle and new tyres on coupled wheels.*
Dar. 19/8-3/10/39.**G.**
Dar. 7/8-18/9/41.**G.**
Dar. 19/11/41-17/1/42.**L.**
Dar. 18/1-9/3/43.**G.**
Cow. 18-20/5/44.**L.**
Cow. 14/2-1/3/45.**G.**
Cow. 7-15/9/45.**L.**
Cow. 14-18/1/46.**L.**

Cow. 12-22/6/46.**L.** *Frames lined up & gauged.*
Dar. 25/6-16/8/47.**G.**
Dar. 16/9-28/10/49.**G.**
Cow. 11-20/5/50.**C/L.**
Dar. 13/8-8/9/51.**G.**
Dar. 19/5-20/6/53.**C/H.**
Dar. 17/3-20/4/55.**G.**
Dar. 2/7/57.*Weigh.*
22/9-18/5/58.*In store at York.*

BOILERS:
1998.
1986 *(ex245)* 7/12/31.
2023 *(ex270)* 7/6/33.
2038 *(ex320)* 2/3/35.
2124 *(ex2755)* 21/3/36.
2603 *(ex322)* 3/10/39.
7963 *(ex236)* 18/9/41.
2627 *(ex320)* 9/3/43.
2174 *(ex277)* 16/8/47.
2654 *(ex2771)* 28/10/49.
2654 Renumbered 27385 8/9/51.
27418 *(ex2709)* 20/4/55.

SHEDS:
Neville Hill.
York 20/7/28.
Hull Botanic Gardens 20/7/32.
Neville Hill 15/5/33.
Hull Botanic Gardens 2/6/39.
Haymarket 2/6/43.
St Margarets 17/11/47.
York 9/3/52.
Neville Hill 17/8/58.

RENUMBERED:
2702 20/10/46.
62702 28/10/49.

CONDEMNED:
12/11/58.

256 HERTFORDSHIRE

Darlington.

To traffic 8/12/27.

REPAIRS:
Dar. 16/1-26/2/29.**N/C.**
Dar. 13/6-5/7/29.**N/C.**
Dar. 8/11/29-22/1/30.**G.**
Dar. 16/5-3/7/30.**N/C.** *After collision.*
Dar. 28/1-27/2/31.**N/C.**
Ghd. 27/7-10/9/31.**L.**
Dar. 20/1-22/3/32.**G.**
Dar. 3/4-12/5/34.**G.**

WORKS CODES:- Cow - Cowlairs. Dar - Darlington. Don - Doncaster. Ghd - Gateshead. Gor - Gorton. Inv - Inverurie. Str - Stratford.
*REPAIR CODES:- **C/H** - Casual Heavy. **C/L** - Casual Light. **G** - General. **H** - Heavy. **H/I** - Heavy Intermediate. **L** - Light. **L/I** - Light Intermediate. **N/C** - Non-Classified.*

11

On the Part 3 engines,the vertical lever drive to the oscillating cams of the poppet valves, needed improvement, and was soon replaced by horizontal lever of Gresley's 2 to 1 gear. Removal of the vertical levers also led to the disappearance of their small box cover. When no.329 INVERNESS-SHIRE came out so altered in June 1929, its running number had been moved from tender to cab side, the latter position having become standard. *R.K.Blencowe*

Dar. 19/9-23/10/35.**L.**
Dar. 15/10/36-14/1/37.**G.**
Heat.conn.at front.
Dar. 30/9-17/11/38.**G.**
Dar. 11/12/40-17/1/41.**G.**
Dar. 13/4-20/5/42.**H/I.**
Cow. 31/12/43-29/1/44.**G.**
Dar. 30/8-19/10/46.**G.**
Dar. 2/11/46-8/2/47.**L.**
Dar. 11-19/2/47.**N/C.**
Ghd. 8/3-2/4/48.**L.**
Dar. 17/3-14/4/49.**G.**
Dar. 13/2-17/3/51.**G.**
Dar. 29-31/3/51.**N/C.**
Dar. 27/11/52-9/1/53.**G.**
Dar. 11/3-15/4/54.**C/H.**
Dar. 1-30/7/54.**H/I.**
Dar. 18/2-21/3/56.**C/L.**
Dar. 25/5-3/8/57.**G.**
29/9-8/12/57.*In store at Botanic Gardens.*

BOILERS:
 2000.
 2024 *(ex311)* 12/5/34.
 2952 *(new)* 17/11/38.
 2947 *(ex322)* 17/1/41.
 2654 *(ex298)* 29/1/44.
 2925 *(ex1460)* 19/10/46.
 3961 *(new)* 14/4/49.
 27367 *(ex2724)* 17/3/51.
 27352 *(ex2755)* 9/1/53.
 27405 *(ex2724)* 15/4/54.

27413 *(ex2767)* 3/8/57.

SHEDS:
Neville Hill.
York 20/7/28.
Hull Botanic Gardens 7/10/36.
Bridlington 12/11/50.
Hull Botanic Gardens 22/9/57.

RENUMBERED:
 2703 12/1/47.
62703 14/4/49.

CONDEMNED:
24/6/58.
Fell into turntable pit at Bridlington 27/5/58.

264 STIRLINGSHIRE

Darlington.

To traffic 14/12/27.

REPAIRS:
Cow. 18/3/29. *For frame crack.*
Dar. 29/2-28/4/32.**G.**
Dar. 31/5-8/6/32. *Tender only.*
Dar. 26/9-2/11/33.**G.**
Cow.6/9/34.**H.**
Dar. 26/4-27/6/35.**H.**
Dar. 18/2-3/4/36.**G.**

Dar. 25/4-6/6/36.**L.**
Dar. 12/3-21/5/37.**G.**
Dar. 29/6-16/9/37.**N/C.**
Cow. 18/7/38.**G.**
Cow. 26/11/38.**L.**
Cow. 13/4/39.**L.**
Cow. 29/11/39.**G.**
Cow. 24/5/41.**G.** *Hudd A.T.C.put on.*
Cow. 7/11/41.**L.**
Cow. 3/10/42.**G.** *Hudd A.T.C.removed.*
Cow. 12/1/43.**L.**
Cow. 3/7/44.**L.**
Cow. 31/3-25/4/45.**G.**
Cow. 28/9/45.**L.**
Cow. 20/10/45.**L.**
Dar. 13/9-24/10/46.**L.** *Smokebox front damage.*
Dar. 5-28/7/47.**L.**
Dar. 7/6-9/7/48.**G.**
Dar. 25/9-27/10/50.**G.**
Dar. 22/10-21/11/53.**H/I.**
Thj. 9-15/12/55.**C/L.**
Dar. 6/3-11/4/56.**G.**
Dar. 11/8/58. *Not repaired.*

BOILERS:
 2002.
 1987 *(ex246)* 2/11/33.
 1983 *(ex246)* 3/4/36.
 2160 *(ex2758)* 21/5/37.
 2160 *(as C1729)* 18/7/38.

 126 *(ex310)* 3/10/42.
 3818 *(new)* 9/7/48.
 27357 *(new)* 27/10/50.
 27435 *(ex2769)* 11/4/56.

SHEDS:
Haymarket.
Perth 10/45.
Thornton Junction 2/2/46.

RENUMBERED:
 2704 24/10/46.
62704 9/7/48.

CONDEMNED:
18/8/58.

265 LANARKSHIRE

Darlington.

To traffic 22/12/27.

REPAIRS:
Cow. 1/30.**G.**
Dar. 8/6-27/7/33.**G.**
Cow.21/8/34.**H.**
Dar. 8/5-5/7/35.**H.**
Dar. 28/2-2/5/36.**G.**
Dar. 28/1-18/3/37.**L.**
Dar. 13/9-19/11/37.**G.**
Heat.conn.at front.

Dar. 22/11-3/12/37.**N/C.**
Cow. 14/7/38.**L.**
Cow. 31/12/38.**G.**
Cow. 26/5/39.**L.**
Cow. 15/10/39.**L.**
Cow. 29/12/39.**L.**
Cow. 1/6/40.**L.**
Cow. 22/11/40.**G.** *Hudd.A.T.C.put on.*
Cow. 24/3/42.**G.** *Hudd.A.T.C.removed.*
Cow. 26/12/42.**L.**
Cow. 9/10/43.**G.**
Cow. 30/9/44.**L.**
Cow. 23/5-17/6/45.**G.**
Dar. 17/8-12/9/46.**L.**
Dar. 14/11-14/12/46.**L.**
Dar. 13/3-11/5/48.**G.**
Dar. 13/11-15/12/50.**L/I.**
Dar. 18-19/12/50.**N/C.**
Dar. 24/8-26/9/53.**G.**
Dar. 15/12/55-20/1/56.**G.**
Dar. 20/11/59. *Not repaired.*

BOILERS:
2012.
1986 *(ex253)* 27/7/33.
2029 *(ex277)* 5/7/35.
2602 *(ex362)* 19/11/37.
3798 *(new)* 11/5/48.
3798 Ren. 27361 15/12/50.
27424 *(ex2754)* 26/9/53.
27356 *(ex2758)* 20/1/56.

SHEDS:
St Margarets.
Haymarket 3/43.

RENUMBERED:
2705 9/12/46.
62705 11/5/48.

CONDEMNED:
30/11/59.

266 FORFARSHIRE

Darlington.

To traffic 28/12/27.

REPAIRS:
Cow. 9/1-18/2/28.**L.** *Washout plugs renewed.*
Dar. 5/11/31-5/1/32.**G.** *New cylinders.*
Dar. 17/3-3/5/33.**G.**
Cow. 9/5-29/6/34.**L.**
Dar. 20/9-30/10/35.**G.**
Dar. 15/1-24/2/37.**G.**
Dar. 22/5-2/7/37.**L.**
Cow. 11/2/38.**L.**
Cow. 10/12/38.**G.**
Cow. 11/11/39.**G.**
Cow. 22/3/40.**L.**
Cow. 28/5/40.**L.**
Cow. 25/12/40.**L.**
Cow. 9/8/41.**G.**
Cow. 23/3/42.**L.**
Cow. 13/3/43.**G.**
Cow. 5/11/43.**L.**
Cow. 19/5/44.**G.**
Cow. 27/12/44.**L.**
Cow. 12-26/5/45.**L.**
Cow. 30/6-12/7/45.**L.**
Cow. 29/10-26/12/45.**G.**
Cow. 13/4-11/5/46.**L.**
Dar. 8/10-9/11/46.**L.**
Dar. 23/5-27/6/47.**L.**
Dar. 21/6-13/8/48.**G.**
Dar. 1-16/9/48.**N/C.**
Dar. 9/12/48-5/1/49. *Special exam.*
Cow. 7-10/12/49.**C/L.**
Dar. 5/2-6/3/52.**G.**
Dar. 12-24/3/52.**N/C.**
Ghd. 5-20/9/52.**C/L.**
Dar. 28/8-10/10/53.**C/H.**
Dar. 27/7-18/9/54.**H/I.**
Dar. 2-14/9/55.**C/L.**
Dar. 4/11-16/12/55.**C/L.**
Dar. 20/12/57. *Not repaired.*

BOILERS:
2019 *(C1653)*
7950 *(ex281)* 30/10/35.
1992 *(ex270)* 24/2/37.
1992 ren. as C1650 10/12/38.
2163 *(as C1730 ex270)* 13/3/43.
3785 *(new)* 13/8/48.
27400 *(ex2717)* 6/3/52.

SHEDS:
Dundee.
Haymarket 12/1/40.
Thornton Junction 25/4/57.

RENUMBERED:
2706 22/9/46.
62706 13/8/48.

CONDEMNED:
3/2/58.

236 LANCASHIRE

Darlington.

To traffic 14/1/28.

REPAIRS:
Dar. 26/6-13/9/29.**G.**
Dar. 14/4-23/6/31.**G.**
Dar. 30/6-31/7/31.**N/C.**
Dar. 8/11-30/12/32.**G.**
Dar. 21/3-3/4/33.**H.**
Dar. 16/2-23/3/34.**G.**
Dar. 26/9-16/11/34.**L.**
Dar. 23/10-6/12/35.**G.**
Dar. 26/8-27/10/36.**G.**
Dar. 9/8-29/10/37.**G.** *Heat.conn.at front.*
Dar. 2/3-18/4/39.**G.**
Dar. 21/2-12/4/40.**L.** *After coll.*
Dar. 25/2-3/4/41.**G.**
Dar. 19/5-19/6/43.**G.**
Cow. 22/1-17/2/45.**G.**
Cow. 21/4-5/5/45.**L.**
Dar. 7/5-28/6/47.**G.**

Dar. 21-22/4/48. *Not repaired.*
Ghd. 22/4-28/5/48.**L.**
Dar. 14/10-10/11/49.**G.**
Dar. 17-25/11/49.**N/C.**
Dar. 1-27/10/51.**G.**
Dar. 6-8/11/51.**N/C.**
Dar. 7/10-7/11/53.**G.**
Dar. 11-14/11/53.**N/C.**
Dar. 21/9-28/10/55.**G.**
Dar. 7/10-8/11/57.**G.**
1/2-14/6/59. *In store Springhead.*
Dar. 7-17/8/59.**C/L.** *3 new tender axles.*

BOILERS:
1985.
2041 *(ex322)* 30/12/32.
2031 *(ex281)* 23/3/34.
2031 Ren. 7953 16/11/34.
7963 *(ex311)* 6/12/35.
2952 *(ex256)* 3/4/41.
1985 *(ex230)* 19/6/43.
2034 *(ex359)* 17/2/45.
3789 *(new)* 28/6/47.
2777 *(ex2710)* 10/11/49.
27386 *(ex2712)* 27/10/51.
27366 *(ex2761)* 7/11/53.
27354 *(ex2725)* 28/10/55.
27439 *(ex2701)* 8/11/57.

SHEDS:
Neville Hill.
Hull Botanic Gardens 31/5/39.
Bridlington 7/8/49.
Hull Botanic Gardens 9/1/55.
Bridlington 29/5/55.
Hull Botanic Gardens 10/6/56.
Bridlington 23/9/56.
Hull Botanic Gardens 22/9/57.
Hull Dairycoates 14/6/59.

RENUMBERED:
2707 12/5/46.
62707 28/5/48.

CONDEMNED:
6/10/59.

The final engine of Part 3 differed from the other five by being fitted with M.L.S. superheater, and a multiple valve regulator located in the smokebox. Despite the engine having left-hand driving position, the regulator control rod was along the right hand side of the boiler. No.335 BEDFORDSHIRE was the first D49 to have its number on the cab side. *T.G.Hepburn*

270 ARGYLLSHIRE

Darlington.

To traffic 20/1/28.

REPAIRS:
Cow. 18/3-5/4/29. Frame crack.
Cow. 9/10/30.**G.**
Dar. 22/10-21/12/31.**G.** Raven fog signal apparatus fitted. New Cylinders.
Dar. 5/4-16/5/33.**G.**
Dar. 6/7-2/8/33.**N/C.**
Dar. 28/9-3/11/34.**G.**
Dar. 1/11/35-29/1/36.**L.**
Dar. 16/11/36-23/1/37.**G.**
Dar. 14/10-19/11/37.**L.**
Cow. 11/12/37.**L.**
Cow. 7/7/38.**H.**
Cow. 14/4/39.**L.**
Cow. 7/10/39.**L.**
Cow. 14/9/40.**G.**
Cow. 30/6/41.**L.**
Cow. 19/12/42.**G.**
Cow. 28/4/43.**L.**
Cow. 1/12/43.**L.**
Cow. 2/8/44.**L.**
Cow. 31/3-25/4/45.**G.**
Cow. 5/1-2/2/46.**L.**
Cow. 4-11/5/46.**L.**
Dar. 26/2-9/8/47.**G.**
Dar. 23/10-12/11/48.**L.**
Dar. 14/11-13/12/49.**G.**
Dar. 11/6-5/7/52.**L/I.**
Dar. 7-9/7/52.**N/C.**
Dar. 8/9-8/10/54.**G.**
Dar. 13-24/2/56.**N/C.**
Dar. 3/9-4/10/56.**G.**
Dar. 23/4/59. Not repaired.

BOILERS:
2023.
1992 (ex250) 16/5/33.
2163 (ex2759) 23/1/37.
2160 (as C1729 ex264) 19/12/42.
4007 (new) 13/12/49.
4007 Renumbered 27415 5/7/52.
27355 (ex2743) 8/10/54.
27420 (ex2716) 4/10/56.

SHEDS:
Haymarket.
Dundee 1/35.
Thornton Junction 2/43.
Perth 6/43.
Thornton Junction 7/43.

RENUMBERED:
2708 14/9/46.
62708 13/12/49.

CONDEMNED:
4/5/59.

277 BERWICKSHIRE

Darlington.

To traffic 24/1/28.

REPAIRS:
Dar. 17-23/2/28.**N/C.**
Dar. 3-21/4/33.**L.**
Dar. 31/7-19/9/33.**G.**
Dar. 5/3-15/4/35.**G.**
Dar. 16/5-10/7/36.**G.**
Dar. 14/1-12/3/37.**L.** After collision.
Dar. 22/10-20/12/37.**G.**
Cow. 22/10/38.**G.**
Cow. 9/3/40.**G.**
Cow. 20/3/41.**L.** Hudd A.T.C.fitted.
Cow. 17/1/42.**G.** Hudd A.T.C.removed.
Cow. 26/3/42.**L.**
Cow. 7/11/42.**L.**
Cow. 8/5/43.**G.**
Cow. 26/11/43.**L.**
Cow. 16/11/44.**L.**
Cow. 28/3-26/4/45.**G.**
Cow. 6/10/45.**L.**
Cow. 2/9/46.**L.**
Dar. 5/6-19/7/47.**G.**
Ghd. 17/11-9/12/48.**L.**
Dar. 7/6-24/9/49.**G.**
Dar. 9-29/12/49.**C/L.**
Dar. 3/7-16/8/52.**H/I.**
Dar. 18-20/8/52.**N/C.**
Dar. 21/4-26/5/54.**C/L.**
Ghd. 14/2-11/3/55.**G.**
Dar. 6/1-6/2/58.**G.**
Dar. 18/12/59. Not repaired.

BOILERS:
2029.
2023 (ex253) 15/4/35.
1996 (ex232) 10/7/36.
2005 (ex307) 20/12/37.
2012 (ex2754) 9/3/40.
1992 (ex266) 8/5/43.
2174 (ex279) 26/4/45.
127 (ex258) 19/7/47.
3998 (new) 24/9/49.
3998 Renumbered 27418 16/8/52.
27414 (ex2732) 11/3/55.
27363 (ex2727) 6/2/58.

SHEDS:
St Margarets.
Perth 4/5/32.
St Margarets 7/33.
Haymarket 3/43.

RENUMBERED:
2709 7/9/46.
62709 9/12/48.

CONDEMNED:
1/1/60.

245 LINCOLNSHIRE

Darlington.

To traffic 7/2/28.

REPAIRS:
Dar. 27/11/28-22/1/29.**L.**
Dar. 23/12/29-18/2/30.**G.**
Dar. 8/4-11/6/31.**G.**
Ghd. 23-31/12/31.**N/C.**
Dar. 24/1-7/3/33.**G.**
Dar. 29/3-10/4/33.**N/C.**
Dar. 31/10/33-9/2/34.**H.** New springs.
Dar. 10/10/34-1/4/35.**G.**
Dar. 22/5-30/6/36.**L.**
Dar. 4/12/36-4/2/37.**G.**
Dar. 7/2-12/5/38.**G.** Heat.conn.at front.
Dar. 12/3-19/4/40.**G.**
Dar. 14/1-18/2/42.**G.**
Dar. 3/8-16/9/43.**G.**
Cow. 21/7-25/8/45.**G.**
Ghd. 25/11-13/12/46.**L.**
Dar. 29/11/47-23/1/48.**G.**
Dar. 11/9-15/10/48.**L.**
Dar. 2/9-4/10/49.**G.**
Dar. 5/9-3/10/51.**G.**
Dar. 2/7-21/8/53.**G.**
Dar. 31/8-23/9/53.**N/C.**
Dar. 28/10-25/11/55.**G.**
Dar. 8-15/10/56.**C/L.**
Dar. 16/5-29/6/57.**G.**
Dar. 27/10-7/11/58.**N/C.**
Dar. 6-8/8/59.**N/C.**
Dar. 8-14/9/59.**C/L.**
Dar. 27/9/60. Not repaired.

BOILERS:
1986.
2332 (new) 11/6/31.
125 (ex288) 1/4/35.
1998 (ex327) 4/2/37.
2151 (ex318) 19/4/40.
7951 (ex2755) 18/2/42.
2952 (ex236) 16/9/43.
2950 (ex258) 25/8/45.
2777 (ex309) 23/1/48.
4000 (new) 4/10/49.
27383 (ex2748) 3/10/51.
27392 (ex2726) 21/8/53.
27351 (ex2736) 25/11/55.
27396 (ex2701) 29/6/57.

SHEDS:
Neville Hill.
Kings Cross 29/9/28.
Neville Hill 29/4/29.
Eastfield 22/9/37.
Neville Hill 28/4/38.
Hull Botanic Gardens 10/6/39.
Bridlington 26/9/54.
Hull Botanic Gardens 9/1/55.
Hull Dairycoates 14/6/59.

RENUMBERED:
2710 13/12/46.
62710 15/10/48.

CONDEMNED:
3/10/60.

281 DUMBARTONSHIRE

Darlington.

To traffic 9/2/28.

REPAIRS:
Cow. 12/29.**G.**
Dar. 10/4-12/6/31.**G.**
Dar. 21/6-18/8/32.**G.** New cyls.
Dar. 31/1-14/3/34.**G.**
Dar. 11/9-18/10/35.**G.**
Dar. 29/7-24/9/36.**H.**
Dar. 13/1-12/3/37.**G.**
Dar. 11/11/37-19/1/38.**G.**
Cow. 6/12/38.**L.**
Cow. 1/7/39.**G.** Hudd A.T.C. fitted.
Cow. 26/3/40.**L.**
Cow. 25/5/40.**L.**
Cow. 26/7/40.**L.**
Cow. 21/12/40.**G.**
Cow. 9/5/42.**G.**
Cow. 6/4/44.**G.**
Cow. 24/5/45.**L.**
Cow. 8/9/45.**L.**
Cow. 2/2/46.**G.**
Cow. 10/5/46.**L.**
Cow. 14/6/46.**L.**
Dar. 20/6-30/8/47.**L.**
Dar. 10/9-15/10/48.**G.**
Dar. 1-8/11/48.**N/C.**
Dar. 12/9-4/11/50.**G.**
Dar. 6-7/11/50.**N/C.**
Dar. 12/11-6/12/52.**L/I.**
Cow. 14-19/6/54.**N/C.**
Cow. 8-16/12/54.**C/L.**
Ghd. 13/4-13/5/55.**G.**
Dar. 25/2-26/3/58.**G.**
Dar. 1-16/4/58.**N/C.**

BOILERS:
2031.
7950 (ex232) 14/3/34.
7949 (ex220) 18/10/35.
C1731 (ex2760) 21/12/40.
C1798 (ex2979) 2/2/46.
2604 (ex2724) 15/10/48.
2604 Ren. 27360 4/11/50.
27436 (new) 13/5/55.
27414 (ex2709) 26/3/58.

SHEDS:
St Margarets.
Haymarket 3/43.
St Margarets 21/3/49.
Hawick 23/4/61.

335's left hand driving position is clearly shown by the rod to its reversing gear. On that side there was only a small cover on the smokebox for the superheater header end. *W.H.Whitworth*

RENUMBERED:
2711 14/9/46.
62711 15/10/48.

CONDEMNED:
1/5/61.
Cut up at Darlington.

246 MORAYSHIRE

Darlington.

To traffic 20/2/28.

REPAIRS:
Cow. 22/2-6/3/28.**N/C.** *Tab exch.fitted.*
Dar. 20/5-17/6/31.**L.**
Dar. 12/10-9/12/31.**L.**
Dar. 21/4-9/6/32.**G.** *New cylinders.*
Dar. 5/9-18/10/33.**G.**
Dar. 1/12/33-20/2/34.**L.**
Dar. 10/1-9/4/35.**H.**
Dar. 18/12/35-2/4/36.**G.** *New frames.*
Dar. 19/3-29/4/37.**G.**
Dar. 12-27/7/37.**N/C.**
Cow. 24/8/38.**H.**
Cow. 30/9/39.**G.**
Cow. 27/12/41.**G.**
Cow. 28/1/42.**L.**
Cow. 18/9/43.**G.**
Cow. 13/7/44.**L.**
Cow. 27/10/44.**L.**
Cow. 17/3/45.**L.**
Cow. 25/5/45.**G.**
Dar. 11/7-12/9/47.**G.**
Dar. 19/12/49-1/2/50.**G.**
Dar. 7-10/2/50.**N/C.**
Dar. 15/8-14/9/51.**G.**

Dar. 17-27/6/53.**C/L.**
Dar. 1/3-2/4/54.**G.**
Dar. 7-10/4/54.**N/C.**
Dar. 21/6-9/8/57.**G.**
Dar. 12-14/8/57.**N/C.**

BOILERS:
1987.
1983 *(ex234)* 18/10/33.
2632 *(ex376)* 2/4/36.
2332 *(ex311)* 27/12/41.
C1655 *(ex306)* 18/9/43.
3806 *(new)* 12/9/47.
3784 *(ex2734)* 1/2/50.
27381 *(ex2723)* 14/9/51.
27397 *(ex2766)* 2/4/54.
27395 *(ex2753)* 9/8/57.

SHEDS:
Dundee.
Perth 8/30.
Haymarket 4/3/44.
St Margarets 22/3/48.
Thornton Junction 27/1/58.
Hawick 4/4/60.

RENUMBERED:
2712 10/11/46.
62712 1/2/50.

CONDEMNED:
3/7/61.
Transferred to S.B. at Slateford Laundry
Sold 6/1/65 for preservation.

249 ABERDEENSHIRE

Darlington.

To traffic 21/2/28.

REPAIRS:
Dar. 30/11/31-8/2/32.**G.** *New cylinders.*
Cow. 4/6/32.**L.**
Dar. 1/2-14/3/34.**G.**
Dar. 23/1-15/3/35.**L.**
Dar. 25/11/35-11/2/36.**G.**
Dar. 20/3-14/5/37.**G.**
Cow. 15/7/38.**N/C.**
Cow. 17/6/39.**N/C.**
Dar. 5-6/4/40. *Not repaired. Sent to Cowlairs.*
Cow. 4/6/40.**G.**
Cow. 31/5/41.**H.**
Cow. 6/12/41.**L.**
Cow. 22/8/42.**G.**
Cow. 14/3/44.**G.**
Cow. 14-21/4/45.**L.**
Cow. 12/1-16/3/46.**G.**
Dar. 27/1-5/3/48.**L.**
Dar. 26/5-23/6/48.**L.**
Dar. 12/9-13/10/49.**G.**
Dar. 19/4-12/5/51.**C/L.**
Dar. 17/6-12/7/52.**H/I.**
Dar. 29/4-29/5/54.**G.**
Dar. 31/5-1/6/54.**N/C.**
Ghd. 22/11-8/12/55.**C/L.**
Dar. 15/6-1/8/56.**G.**

BOILERS:
1990.
1983 *(ex264)* 14/5/37.
2616 *(ex2756)* 31/5/41.
2768 *(ex298)* 16/3/46.
4001 *(new)* 13/10/49.
4001 *Renumbered* 27416 12/7/52.
27350 *(ex2720)* 29/5/54.
27386 *(ex2724)* 1/8/56.

SHEDS:
Dundee.
Thornton Junction 5/11/50.

RENUMBERED:
2713 14/9/46.
E2713 5/3/48.
62713 23/6/48.

CONDEMNED:
9/9/57.

250 PERTHSHIRE

Darlington.

To traffic 2/3/28.

REPAIRS:
Dar. 2/3-29/4/31.**G.**
Dar. 3/12/31-5/2/32.**L.**
Dar. 7/3-11/5/33.**G.** *New cylinders.*
Dar. 2/10-15/11/34.**G.**
Dar. 11/9-20/12/35.**G.** *New frames.*
Dar. 18/6-19/8/36.**L.**
Dar. 8/3-17/4/37.**G.**
Dar. 22/10/37-6/1/38.**H.**
Cow. 29/10/38.**G.**
Cow. 3/3/39.**L.**
Cow. 15/11-7/12/39.**L.**
Cow. 19/9-12/10/40.**G.**
Cow. 20/2-30/4/42.**G.**
Cow. 10/3/43.**L.**
Cow. 4/12/43.**G.**
Cow. 27/1/44.**L.**
Cow. 4/4/44.**L.**
Cow. 18/7/44.**L.**
Cow. 18/12/44.**L.**
Cow. 17/2-17/3/45.**G.**
Cow. 3-24/11/45.**L.**
Dar. 14/12/46-29/3/47.**G.**
Ghd. 30/9-27/10/48.**L.**
Dar. 7/7-31/8/49.**G.**
Dar. 9/4-12/5/51.**G.**
Dar. 25/3-9/5/53.**G.**

The next D49s into traffic were eight of Part 1, numbered 2753 to 2760, completed in February to June 1929. They had three visible differences from the later engines of the first twenty Part 1, being fitted with screw instead of steam reversing gear, not having equipment for air braking, and their tenders were flush sided. Two other differences were not discernible; their boiler tubes had Diamond soot blowers, and seven of them had Owen double-beat regulator, the other, no.2754 being fitted with a 'Joco' type. *WBY collection.*

Although included in the original order placed in 1926 for 28 engines, the last two did not enter traffic until 1929, and when no.352 LEICESTERSHIRE was new in March, it had Lentz poppet valves operated by rotary cam gear, and initiated Part 2 of the class. It was akin to Part 1 in being fitted with Westinghouse air brake and stepped top tender. *W.L.Good*

Dar. 16/7-13/9/54.**C**/**L**.
Dar. 4/7-5/8/55.**G**.
Dar. 17-29/4/57.**N/C**.
Dar. 4/7-17/8/57.**G**.
Ghd. 15-31/10/58.**C/L**.

BOILERS:
 1992.
 2148 *(ex2755)* 11/5/33.
 2002 *(ex251)* 20/12/35.
 2019 *(ex211)* 17/4/37.
 2019 *(C1653)* 29/10/38.
C1658 *(ex2753)* 30/4/42.
 2613 *(ex214)* 17/3/45.
 2613 Ren.27376 12/5/51.
27367 *(ex2703)* 9/5/53.
27421 *(ex2718)* 5/8/55.
27405 *(ex2703)* 17/8/57.

SHEDS:
Perth.
Stirling 9/9/51.

RENUMBERED:
 2714 10/11/46.
62714 27/10/48.

CONDEMNED:
26/8/59.
Cut up at Darlington.

306 ROXBURGHSHIRE

Darlington.

To traffic 6/3/28.

REPAIRS:
Cow. 11/29.**G**.
Dar. 27/4-7/7/33.**G**. *New cylinders.*
Dar. 14/6-21/7.**G**.
Dar. 6/6-6/8/35.**G**.
Dar. 7/10-26/11/36.**G**.
Dar. 1/3-13/4/37.**H**.
Dar. 9/11/37-7/1/38.**G**.
Cow. 23/6/39.**L**.

Cow. 22/2/40.**G**.
Cow. 12/7/40.**L**.
Cow. 4/10/41.**G**.
Cow. 8/8/42.**L**.
Cow. 26/10/42.**L**.
Cow. 1/4/43.**L**.
Cow. 28/8/43.**G**.
Cow. 18/2/44.**L**.
Cow. 9/3/45.**G**.
Cow. 23/3/45.**L**.
Cow. 16/10/45.**L**.
Cow. 22/2/46.**L**.
Cow. 27/7/46.**G**.
Dar. 7/5-15/8/47.**L**.
Dar. 24/10-24/11/47.**L**.
Dar. 13/11/48-29/1/49.**G**.
Dar. 7-8/2/49.**N/C**.
Cow. 24-25/11/50.**C/L**.
Dar. 19/4-24/5/51.**G**.
Dar. 9-30/10/51.**C/L**.
Cow. 3-5/7/52.**N/C**.
Ghd. 22/12/52-17/1/53.**C/L**.
Dar. 1-27/2/54.**G**.
Dar. 10/1-18/2/57.**C/L**.
Dar. 4/12/57-14/1/58.**G**.

Dar. 15-20/5/58.**N/C**.
Dar. 23/6/59. *Not repaired.*

BOILERS:
 2009.
 2046 *(ex309)* 26/11/36.
 2029 *(ex265)* 7/1/38.
 2598 *(ex309)* 28/8/43.
 7964 *(ex374)* 29/1/49.
27373 *(ex2722)* 24/5/51.
27402 *(ex2721)* 27/2/54.
27386 *(ex2713)* 14/1/58.

SHEDS:
St Margarets.
Haymarket 3/43.
St Margarets 17/11/47.

RENUMBERED:
 2715 17/11/46.
62715 29/1/49.

CONDEMNED:
29/6/59.

No. 336 BUCKINGHAMSHIRE completed the first order when new in June 1929, and differed from 352 only by name and number. Although the rotating drive for the valve gear was on the right hand side, the driver's control rod was on the left hand side. *J.J.Cunningham*

The class total remained at 36 (28 Part 1, 2 Part 2, and 6 Part 3) until April 1932, and then by October, it had been augmented by another ten Part 2, that variety having been adopted as the best for further construction. Those ten took vacant numbers in the 201 to 282 range, and were allocated to N.E.Area. Cowlairs works built the boilers for them, and fitted four washout plugs instead of two handholes on both sides. Darlington added a new item by fitting them with hinged glass sight screen between the cab windows, and their tenders had been built in 1926 for J38 class, which explains why they had stepped top. They were named for Hunts, that having been adopted as standard for Part 2. *W.L.Good*

Although showing no external evidence of difference, the last of the batch, no.282 THE HURWORTH was fitted with a camshaft giving variable cut-off from 15 to 84%, whereas on the other nine, there were just five fixed positions in forward gear. That special camshaft was replaced in March 1934 by one having seven fixed positions which, by then, had become the standard. *J.G.Gregory*

Five more Part 2 with numbers from 283 to 298 went into traffic during August and September 1933. Their boilers had four washout plugs on each side, but had been built 'across the road' by R.Stephenson's Darlington works. Second-hand tenders from J38 class were coupled with them, and on the engines, further use was made of Woodard connecting rods. *J.G.Gregory*

The total finally reached 76, by the building of a batch of 25 between July 1934 and February 1935 with numbers taking vacancies from 205 to 377, and as with all Part 2, they were allocated to N.E.Area. For them Darlington works built the boilers, the flush sided tenders, and provided them with seven-position cams. The first twenty (to no.368) did not have train heating connection fitted at the front end when they were new. *Photomatic*

The Scottish Area drivers disliked the steam reverse fitted on the 14 Part 1 engines sent to that Area, and lobbied sufficiently to have it replaced by screw type. In March/April 1929 Cowlairs works altered three nos 270, 250, and 264 using an arrangement they devised with a straight rod and an exit from the cab which put the rod above the nameplate.

From June 1929 to June 1932 Cowlairs then altered the other eleven from steam to screw operated reversing gear. For those they had worked to a Darlington drawing which had a rod with downward curve at both ends, and at a lower level, which put it *behind* the nameplate. The six Part 1 allocated to North Eastern Area continued to use steam reverse without difficulty until Darlington accepted that, with screw a more precise position could be set, and maintained. Then, from April 1935 (no.245) to January 1937 (no.256) those six were changed to screw, and with their design of operating rod. *J.G.Gregory*

From 16th October 1928 until it went to works in April 1930, Part 1 no.251 DERBYSHIRE was fitted with a Kylala blast pipe, but retained its single chimney, so that item made no discernible difference externally. *Real Photos*

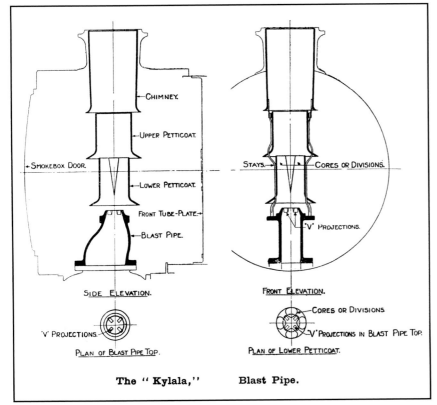

The " Kylala," Blast Pipe.

(upper left) **In the Kylala arrangement, the top of the blast pipe was fitted with four projections to split the exhaust steam flow, and assist its fluidity.** *LNER*

(upper right) **Photograph showing how the lower petticoat was suspended in the smokebox. There was no indication externally to show when this device was installed.** *LNER*

(left) **This line diagram shows front and side sectional views of the petticoat arrangement inside the smokebox for the Kylala trial.** *LNER*

To compare performance between Parts 1 and 3, from 17th April 1929 until June 1930, Part 3 no.322 HUNTINGDONSHIRE was fitted with the same Kylala arrangement, but the trials carried out from Leeds Neville Hill shed were then terminated, without any subsequent effect on D49 class.

307 KINCARDINESHIRE

Darlington.

To traffic 17/3/28.

REPAIRS:
Dar. 7/4-2/6/32.**G.** *New cylinders.*
Dar. 1/3-20/4/34.**G.**
Dar. 25/6-6/8/35.**L.**
Dar. 15/2-9/4/36.**G.**
Dar. 3/5-21/6/37.**L.**
Dar. 22/9-1/12/37.**G.**
Dar. 9/5-4/8/38. *Not repaired. Sent to Cowlairs.*
Cow. 26/8/38.**L.**
Cow. 20/5/39.**L.**
Cow. 16/9/39.**L.**
Cow. 23/3/40.**L.**
Cow. 26/2/41.**G.**
Cow. 28/8/42.**G.**
Cow. 16/7/43.**L.**
Cow. 23/10/43.**G.**
Cow. 1/6/44.**L.**
Cow. 11/11/44.**L.**
Cow. 2/6/45.**L.**
Cow. 14/12/45.**G.**
Dar. 8/8-12/9/47.**G.**
Dar. 26/9-2/10/47.**N/C.**
Dar. 18/11-20/12/49.**G.**
Dar. 5-13/7/50.**C/L.**
Inv. 9/12/50.**C/L.**
Cow. 26-29/9/51.**N/C.**
Inv. 2-8/7/52.**N/C.**
Dar. 30/10-22/11/52.**G.**
Dar. 24/11-5/12/52.**N/C.**
Dar. 16/7-14/8/54.**G.**
Thj. 12-29/9/55.**C/L.**
Thj. 24/1-22/2/56.**C/L.**
Thj. 12-19/3/56.**C/L.**
Dar. 10/7-28/8/56.**G.**

BOILERS:
2005.
7948 *(ex251)* 1/12/37.
2710 *(ex1456)* 23/10/43.
3786 *(new)* 12/9/47.
2174 *(ex2702)* 20/12/49.
27363 *(ex2772)* 22/11/52.
27420 *(ex2735)* 14/8/54.
27379 *(ex2774)* 28/8/56.

SHEDS:
Dundee.
Aberdeen 1/31.
Dundee 1/33.
Thornton Junction 2/43.
St Margarets 18/4/60.

RENUMBERED:
2716 27/10/46.
62716 20/12/49.

CONDEMNED:
28/4/61.

309 BANFFSHIRE

Darlington.

To traffic 26/3/28.

REPAIRS:
Cow. 4/4-12/5/28.**N/C.** *Tablet app.fitted.*
Cow. 11/4-30/5/30.**G.**
Cow. 11/9-4/10/30.**L.**
Dar. 5/3-11/5/31.**G.**
Dar. 17/5-18/6/32.**H.** *New cylinders.*
Dar. 2/11/32-11/1/33.**G.**
Dar. 27/12/33-5/1/34.**L.**
Dar. 30/1-27/2/34.**L.**
Dar. 29/5-11/7/34.**G.**
Dar. 4/9-1/11/34.**H.**
Dar. 16/7-12/9/35.**G.**
Dar. 17/8-24/10/36.**G.**
Dar. 31/5-17/8/37.**L.**
Cow. 19-23/11/37.**L.**
Dar. 29/4-10/6/38.**G.**
Cow. 2-10/3/39.**L.**
Cow. 30/8-2/10/39.**L.**
Cow. 25-29/4/40.**L.**
Cow. 22/1-25/2/41.**H.** *Hudd A.T.C.fitted.*
Cow. 23/1-10/2/42.**L.** *Hudd A.T.C. removed.*
Cow. 12/5-13/6/42.**G.**
Cow. 30/6-6/7/42.**L.**
Cow. 27/5-19/6/43.**H.**
Cow. 25/5-7/6/44.**L.**
Cow. 25/8-12/9/44.**L.**
Cow. 7-27/3/45.**H.**
Cow. 2-24/4/46.**L.**
Dar. 17/10-9/12/46.**L.**
Dar. 26/6-28/8/47.**G.**
Dar. 7/2-22/4/50.**G.**
Dar. 29/11/51-4/1/52.**G.**
Dar. 18/1-1/2/52.**N/C.**
Dar. 21/10-20/11/53.**G.**
Dar. 18/1-23/2/55.**G.**
Dar. 31/7-5/9/56.**G.**
Dar. 23/4-6/6/58.**G.**
Dar. 13/1/61. *Not repaired.*

BOILERS:
2014.
1985 *(ex236)* 5/1/34.
2046 *(ex2754)* 12/9/35.
2598 *(ex226)* 24/10/36.
2012 *(ex277)* 19/6/43.
2777 *(ex292)* 9/12/46.
3800 *(new)* 28/8/47.
2603 *(ex2740)* 22/4/50.
27426 *(new)* 4/1/52.
27395 *(ex2769)* 20/11/53.

27417 *(ex2727)* 23/2/55.
27373 *(ex2734)* 5/9/56.
27422 *(ex2718)* 6/6/58.

SHEDS:
Dundee.
Eastfield 4/10/30.
Haymarket 4/2/31.
Thornton Junction 12/12/43.
Hull Botanic Gardens 1/1/51.
Hull Dairycoates 14/6/59.

RENUMBERED:
2717 9/12/46.
62717 22/4/50.

CONDEMNED:
13/1/61.

310 KINROSS-SHIRE

Darlington.

To traffic 3/5/28.

REPAIRS:
Cow. 31/5/28. **N/C.** *Tablet app. fitted.*
Dar. 14/6-18/8/32.**G.** *New crank axle & cyls.*
Dar. 14/11/33-8/2/34.**G.**
Dar. 27/8-4/10/34.**H.**
Dar. 8/2-19/3/36.**G.**
Dar. 18/11/36-19/2/37.**G.**
Dar. 8/10-9/12/37.**L.**
Cow. 7/10/38.**L.**
Cow. 20/10/39.**L.**
Cow. 1/9/40.**L.**
Cow. 11/4/41.**G.**
Cow. 25/7/42.**G.**
Cow. 29/8/42.**L.**
Cow. 9/3/43.**L.**
Cow. 6/11/43.**G.**
Cow. 17/4/44.**L.**
Cow. 19/3/45.**L.**
Cow. 8/6/45.**L.**
Cow. 27/7/46.**H.**
Dar. 27/1-19/3/48.**L.**
Dar. 27/11/48-15/1/49.**G.**
Dar. 25/1-5/2/49.**N/C.**
Dar. 17/7-30/8/52.**H/I.**
Dar. 1-6/9/52.**N/C.**
Ghd. 10/7-15/8/53.**C/L.**
Dar. 26/5-2/7/55.**G.**
Dar. 4-16/7/55.**N/C.**
Dar. 26/10-15/11/56.**C/L.**
Dar. 28/2-3/4/58.**G.**
Dar. 8-9/4/58.**N/C.**

BOILERS:
2017.
126 *(ex292)* 19/2/37.
1986 *(ex329)* 25/7/42.

4966 *(new)* 15/1/49.
4966 *Ren.*27421 30/8/52.
27422 *(ex2726)* 2/7/55.
27427 *(ex2728)* 3/4/58.

SHEDS:
Dundee.
Aberdeen 1/31.
Dundee 1/33.
St Margarets 9/3/52.

RENUMBERED:
2718 8/12/46.
E2718 19/3/48.
62718 15/1/49.

CONDEMNED:
24/4/61.
Cut up at Darlington.

311 PEEBLES-SHIRE

Darlington.

To traffic 5/5/28.

REPAIRS:
Dar. 19/1-14/4/32.**G.** *New cylinders.*
Dar. 26/3-2/5/34.**G.** *New cylinders.*
Dar. 10/10-22/11/35.**G.**
Dar. 7/10-2/12/36.**G.**
Dar. 5/11-30/12/37.**L.**
Cow. 2/12/38.**G.**
Cow. 30/6/39.**L.**
Cow. 12/7/40.**G.**
Cow. 22/2/41.**L.**
Cow. 6/12/41.**G.**
Cow. 7/11/42.**L.**
Cow. 20/3/43.**L.**
Cow. 16/11/43.**G.**
Cow. 25/2/44.**L.**
Cow. 18/10/44.**L.**
Cow. 18/2/45.**L.**
Cow. 16/8/45.**L.**
Cow. 11/8/45.**L.**
Cow. 27/4/46.**G.**
Dar. 16-24/5/47.**L.**
Dar. 22/8-3/10/47.**L.**
Dar. 11/1-4/3/49.**G.**
Dar. 4-29/6/51.**G.**
Dar. 14/10-21/11/53.**H/I.**
Dar. 23-24/11/53.**N/C.**
Dar. 13/2-13/3/56.**G.**
Dar. 9/12/59. *Not repaired.*

BOILERS:
2024.
7953 *(ex255)* 2/5/34.
2148 *(ex250)* 22/11/35.
2332 *(2753)* 12/7/40.
2605 *(ex2757)* 6/12/41.

WORKS CODES:- Cow - Cowlairs. Dar - Darlington. Don - Doncaster. Ghd - Gateshead. Gor - Gorton. Inv - Inverurie. Str - Stratford.
REPAIR CODES:- C/H - Casual Heavy. C/L - Casual Light. G - General. H - Heavy. H/I - Heavy Intermediate. L - Light. L/I - Light Intermediate. N/C - Non-Classified.

The 36 built to June 1929 (28 Part 1, 2 Part 2, and 6 Part 3) were not fitted with gear to rock the front of the grate when they were new. Note no. 256 therefore does not have inclined rod in front of the cab on the right hand side. From what can be read on its front end notice, it has worked a football excursion to London, and is at King's Cross shed. They have clearly taken no risk of it running short of coal on its 188 mile trip back to York, and one return destination is seen to be Saltburn. *WBY collection*

2249 (*ex1896*) 4/3/49.
27378 (*ex2700*) 29/6/51.
27393 (*ex2757*) 13/3/56.

SHEDS:
St Margarets.
Haymarket 3/43.
Hawick 2/11/59.

RENUMBERED:
2719 14/9/46.
62719 4/3/49.

CONDEMNED:
1/1/60.

318 CAMBRIDGESHIRE

Darlington.

To traffic 7/5/28.

REPAIRS:
Dar. 17/9-1/10/29.**N/C.**
Dar. 19/11/29-4/2/30.**G.** *To 2 to 1 lever.*
Dar. 6/10-1/12/31.**G.**
Dar. 18-23/12/31.**N/C.**
Dar. 10/3-28/4/33.**G.**

Dar. 4/1-14/3/35.**G.** *Heat.conn.at front.*
Dar. 24/9-11/12/35.**L.** *After collision.*
Dar. 17/1-18/3/38.**G.** *Rebuild to piston valve.*
Dar. 21/3-6/4/38.**N/C.**
Dar. 10/8-6/10/39.**G.**
Dar. 26/11/41-3/1/42.**G.**
Dar. 20/4-17/5/43.**L.**
Cow. 3/5-10/6/44.**G.**
Cow. 3-24/3/45.**L.**
Cow. 29/6-3/8/46.**G.**
Ghd. 13/2-7/3/48.**L.**
Dar. 31/3-7/5/49.**G.**
Dar. 12-19/5/49.**N/C.**
Dar. 7-28/6/50.**C/L.**
Dar. 20/2-17/3/51.**G.**
Dar. 23-26/7/51.**C/L.**
Dar. 12/9-24/10/52.**G.**
Dar. 28/5-8/7/53.**C/H.** *New cyls.*
Dar. 12/2-27/3/54.**G.**
Dar. 29/3-13/4/54.**N/C.**
Dar. 2-7/4/55.**C/L.**
Dar. 15/9-14/10/55.**G.**
Dar. 21/2-22/3/57.**G.**

BOILERS:
2034.
2151 (*ex2756*) 14/3/35.

2124 (*ex253*) 6/10/39.
7947 (*ex251*) 3/1/42.
2947 (*ex256*) 10/6/44.
3965 (*new*) 7/5/49.
27368 (*ex2729*) 17/3/51.
27350 (*ex2757*) 24/10/52.
27398 (*ex2756*) 27/3/54.
27426 (*ex2737*) 14/10/55.
27380 (*ex2770*) 22/3/57.

SHEDS:
Neville Hill.
Hull Botanic Gardens 19/5/32.
Bridlington 11/2/35.
Hull Botanic Gardens 22/5/35.
Bridlington 11/7/38.
Hull Botanic Gardens 12/6/39.
Scarborough 15/10/42.
Hull Botanic Gardens 2/6/43.
Hull Dairycoates 14/6/59.

RENUMBERED:
2720 1/12/46.
62720 7/5/49.

CONDEMNED:
6/10/59.

320 WARWICKSHIRE

Darlington.

To traffic 23/5/28.

REPAIRS:
Dar. 12/2-11/3/29.**N/C.**
Dar. 30/4-13/5/29.**N/C.**
Dar. 1/1-13/3/30.**G.** *To 2 to 1 lever.*
Dar. 8/1-10/2/31.**H.**
Dar. 10/11/31-8/1/32.**G.**
Dar. 20/4-7/6/33.**G.**
Dar. 27/12/34-15/3/35.**G.** *Heat.conn.at front.*
Dar. 15/12/37-18/3/38.**G.** *Rebuilt to piston valve.*
Dar. 18/4-21/5/40.**G.**
Dar. 21-31/5/40.**N/C.**
Dar. 14/5-13/6/42.**G.**
Dar. 22/2-19/3/43.**H.**
Cow. 15/7/44.**G.**
Cow. 25/4/45.**G.**
Dar. 27/4/46.**L.** *Rear sanders fitted.*
Dar. 13/9-12/10/46.**L.**
Dar. 29/5-16/7/47.**L.**
Dar. 31/1-19/3/49.**G.**
Dar. 23-24/3/49.**N/C.**
Dar. 29/12/51-1/2/52.**H/I.**

Dar. 5-8/2/52.**N/C.**
Cow. 4-11/3/52.**C/L.**
Dar. 20/11-19/12/53.**G.**
Dar. 4-5/1/54.**N/C.**
Cow. 10-12/3/55.**C/L.**
Dar. 7/2-8/3/56.**G.**
Dar. 6-27/11/57.**C/L.**
Dar. 16/8/58. *Not repaired.*

BOILERS:
  2038.
  2164 *(ex234)* 15/3/35.
  2627 *(ex234)* 21/5/40.
  7964 *(ex377)* 13/6/42.
  2164 *(ex322)* 19/3/43.
  2632 *(ex2728)* 19/3/49.
  2632 Renumbered 27402 1/2/52.
  27390 *(ex2763)* 19/12/53.
  27424 *(ex2705)* 8/3/56.

SHEDS:
York.
Neville Hill 20/7/28.
Hull Botanic Gardens 19/5/32.
Bridlington 17/4/35.
Hull Botanic Gardens 30/5/39.
Haymarket 2/6/43.
St Margarets 22/3/48.

RENUMBERED:
  2721 8/12/46.
  62721 19/3/49.

CONDEMNED:
18/8/58.

322 HUNTINGDONSHIRE

Darlington.

To traffic 10/7/28.

REPAIRS:
Dar. 26/3-17/4/29.**N/C.** *Kylala blast pipe fit.*
Ghd. 9-25/10/29.**L.**
Dar. 13/6-11/9/30.**G.** *Kylala blastpipe off. To 2 to 1 lever.*
Dar. 18/5-25/7/32.**G.**
Dar. 24/4-8/6/34.**G.**
Dar. 28/2-30/4/36.**G.**

Dar. 15/9-18/11/38.**G.** *Rebuilt to piston valve.*
Dar. 3/7-3/8/40.**G.**
Dar. 16/4-30/5/42.**G.**
Cow. 24/5-1/7/44.**G.**
Dar. 12/10-23/11/46.**G.**
Ghd. 26/10-12/11/47.**L.**
Dar. 5-28/5/48.**L.**
Dar. 13/1-5/2/49.**L.** *After collision.*
Dar. 6/7-6/9/49.**G.**
Dar. 17/3-6/4/51.**G.**
Dar. 9-10/4/51.**N/C.**
Dar. 14/1-13/2/53.**G.**
Dar. 18/3-5/5/54.**C/L.**
Ghd. 18/12/54-21/1/55.**G.**
Dar. 28/12/56-6/2/57.**G.**
Dar. 1/8-4/9/57.**C/H.**

BOILERS:
  2041.
  2044 *(ex327)* 25/7/32.
  2044 Renumbered 7954.
  7964 *(ex269)* 8/6/34.
  2603 *(ex279)* 30/4/36.
  2947 *(new)* 18/11/38.
  2164 *(ex320)* 3/8/40.
  1998 *(ex327)* 30/5/42.
  2599 *(ex370)* 23/11/46.
  2953 *(ex364)* 6/9/49.
  27370 *(ex2720)* 6/4/51.
  27406 *(ex2716)* 13/2/53.
  27419 *(ex2730)* 21/1/55.
  27384 *(ex2745)* 6/2/57.

SHEDS:
York.
Neville Hill 20/7/28.
Hull Botanic Gardens 19/5/32.
Hull Dairycoates 14/6/59.

RENUMBERED:
  2722 23/11/46.
  62722 28/5/48.

CONDEMNED:
20/10/59.

327 NOTTINGHAMSHIRE

Darlington.

To traffic 11/7/28.

REPAIRS:
Dar. 11/4-14/5/29.**N/C.**
Dar. 28/3-19/6/30.**G.** *To 2 to 1 lever.*
Dar. 14/1-10/3/32.**G.**
Dar. 31/1-7/3/33.**H.**
Dar. 17/7-11/8/33.**L.**
Dar. 15/3-24/4/34.**G.**
Dar. 30/4-2/5/34.**N/C.**
Dar. 8/6-6/8/36.**G.** *Heat.conn.at front.*
Dar. 28/3-9/6/38.**G.** *Rebuilt to piston valve.*
Dar. 23/3-30/4/40.**G.**
Dar. 18/3-25/4/42.**G.**
Cow. 11/2-18/3/44.**G.**
Cow. 30/1-10/3/45.**G.**
Dar. 26/10-30/11/46.**G.**
Ghd. 29/1-20/2/48.**L.**
Dar. 17/9-15/10/48.**G.**
Dar. 29/6-11/8/50.**G.**
Dar. 21-24/8/50.**N/C.**
Dar. 29/4-23/5/52.**G.**
Dar. 22/1-19/2/54.**G.**
Dar. 12/10-11/11/55.**G.**
Dar. 1-9/11/56.**C/L.**
Dar. 31/7-4/9/57.**G.**
Dar. 9-18/9/57.**N/C.**

BOILERS:
  2044.
  1998 *(ex253)* 10/3/32.
  2154 *(ex234)* 6/8/36.
  1998 *(ex245)* 30/4/40.
  128 *(ex363)* 25/4/42.
  7964 *(ex320)* 18/3/44.
  7951 *(ex364)* 30/11/46.
  126 *(ex2704)* 15/10/48.
  3806 *(ex2712)* 11/8/50.
  27410 *(ex2745)* 23/5/52.
  27376 *(ex2714)* 19/2/54.

27370 *(ex2729)* 11/11/55.
27397 *(ex2712)* 4/9/57.

SHEDS:
York.
Hull Botanic Gardens 19/5/32.
Hull Dairycoates 14/6/59.

RENUMBERED:
  2723 30/11/46.
  62723 15/10/48.

CONDEMNED:
16/1/61.
Cut up at Darlington.

335 BEDFORDSHIRE

Darlington.

To traffic 28/8/28.

REPAIRS:
Dar. 28/1-25/2/29.**N/C.**
Dar. 15/3-23/5/30.**G.** *To 2 to 1 lever.*
Dar. 8/2-4/4/32.**G.**
Dar. 5/10-23/11/34.**G.**
Dar. 11/11/36-7/1/37.**G.**
Dar. 26/8-10/11/38.**G.** *Re-built to piston valve.*
Dar. 15/11-28/12/40.**G.**
Dar. 22/6-13/8/43.**G.** *M.L.S.regulator off.*
Cow. 28/7-22/9/45.**G.**
Cow. 13-27/4/46.**L.**
Ghd. 18/12/46-14/1/47.**L.**
Dar. 14/4-28/5/48.**G.**
Dar. 4-11/6/48.**N/C.**
Dar. 20/6-8/8/49.**G.**
Dar. 2/2-1/3/51.**G.**
Ghd. 28/1-20/2/52.**C/L.**
Ghd. 21-29/2/52.**N/C.**
Dar. 24/6-16/8/52.**G.**
Dar. 18-19/8/52.**N/C.**
Dar. 2-20/3/53.**C/L.**

The 36 engines not at first fitted for rocking the grate, or with hinged glass sight screen cab side, were duly so equipped from 1932, when those two items were standard equipment from the start on the forty Part 2 engines from 201 onwards. *R.C.Copeman*

Dar. 19/11-30/12/53.**C/H.**
Dar. 17/5-19/6/54.**H/I.**
Dar. 20/12/55-23/1/56.**G.**
Dar. 15/10-28/11/56.**C/L.**

BOILERS:
  2051.
  2604 *(ex353)* 7/1/37.
  3815 *(new)* 28/5/48.
  3978 *(new)* 8/8/49.
  27353 *(ex2736)* 1/3/51.
  27405 *(ex2701)* 16/8/52.
  27386 *(ex2707)* 30/12/53.
  27828 *(new)* 23/1/56.

SHEDS:
York.
Hull Botanic Gardens 8/6/32.
Bridlington 17/4/35.
Hull Botanic Gardens 30/5/39.

RENUMBERED:
  2724 15/12/46.
62724 28/5/48.

CONDEMNED:
17/12/57.

329 INVERNESS-SHIRE

Darlington.

To traffic 30/8/28.

REPAIRS:
Dar. 22/10-5/11/28.**N/C.**
Dar. 16/1-1/2/29.**N/C.**
Dar. 26/3-12/6/29.**L.** *To 2 to 1 lever.*
Dar. 23/9-14/10/29.**N/C.**
Dar. 16-30/10/29.**N/C.** *Raven F.S.A.fitted.*
Dar. 17/11/30-30/1/31.**G.**
Dar. 20/1-10/3/33.**G.**
Dar. 10/4-19/5/34.**H.**
Dar. 10/12/34-31/1/35.**G.**
Dar. 24/9/35-9/1/36.**L.**
Dar. 13-16/6/36.**N/C.**
Dar. 19/6-14/10/36.**L.**
Dar. 16-19/10/36.**N/C.**
Dar. 22/5-28/7/37.**H.**
Dar. 30/4-2/9/38.**G.** *Rebuilt to piston valve.*
Cow. 3/6/39.**N/C.** *Hudd ATC fitted.*
Cow. 16/3/40.**G.**
Cow. 19/4/41.**N/C.**
Cow. 15/6/42.**G.** *Hudd A.T.C. removed.*
Cow. 26/3/43.**L.**
Cow. 7/8/43.**H.**
Cow. 15/3-15/4/44.**G.**
Cow. 3/6/44.**L.**

Cow. 18/11/44.**L.**
Cow. 29/9-20/10/45.**G.**
Cow. 28/9-12/10/46.**L.**
Ghd. 26/4-14/5/47.**L.**
Dar. 18/11/47-2/1/48.**G.**
Dar. 21/9-4/11/49.**C/L.**
Cow. 30/3-1/4/50.**C/L.**
Dar. 5/10-7/11/50.**G.**
Ghd. 6-30/10/52.**C/L.**
Dar. 26/8-29/9/53.**L/I.**
Pth. 6/9-5/10/54.**C/L.**
Ghd. 9/8-7/10/55.**G.**
Dar. 21-23/8/56.**C/L.**
Dar. 21-29/1/57.**C/L.**
Dar. 4/11/58. *Not repaired.*

BOILERS:
  2046.
  2014 *(ex309)* 10/3/33.
  1986 *(ex2754)* 28/7/37.
  2019 *(ex250)* 15/6/42.
   128 *(ex327)* 15/4/44.
  2710 *(ex307)* 2/1/48.
  27354 *(new)* 7/11/50.
  27367 *(ex2714)* 7/10/55.

SHEDS:
Perth.
York 22/10/28.
Perth 14/7/29.
York 20/9/29.
Perth 19/2/31.
Eastfield 2/31.
York 29/7/37.
Eastfield 28/4/38.
Thornton Junction 6/38.
Perth 20/5/40.
Stirling 19/10/53.
Stirling (South) 7/2/56.

RENUMBERED:
  2725 15/12/46.
62725 4/11/49.

CONDEMNED:
10/11/58.

352 LEICESTERSHIRE
THE MEYNELL (from 8/6/32)

Darlington.

To traffic 15/3/29.

REPAIRS:
Dar. 8/4-23/8/29.**N/C.**
Dar. 28/10-15/11/29.**N/C.**
Dar. 10/3-19/5/31.**G.**
Dar. 30/5-7/6/32.**N/C.** *for re-naming*
Dar. 23/2-4/5/33.**G.**
Dar. 27/9-22/12/34.**G.**
Dar. 5/6-28/9/36.**G.**

Dar. 8-21/6/37.**N/C.** *Heat.conn.at front.*
Dar. 30/5-18/8/38.**G.**
Dar. 24-25/8/38.**N/C.**
Dar. 5/5-29/6/39.**N/C.**
Dar. 8/5-14/6/41.**G.**
Dar. 1-17/12/41.**H.**
Dar. 27/7-7/9/42.**L.**
Cow. 18/1-11/3/44.**G.**
Cow. 9/8-2/9/44.**L.**
Cow. 26/1-24/2/45.**L.**
Cow. 20/4-15/6/46.**L.**
Dar. 25/11-24/12/47.**L.**
Ghd. 31/1-25/2/48.**L.**
Dar. 13/5-17/6/49.**G.**
Dar. 9/1-6/2/52.**G.**
Dar. 9/2-25/4/53.**G.**
Dar. 30/11-22/12/53.**C/L.**
Dar. 1-26/2/55.**G.**
Dar. 7-19/3/55.**N/C.**
Dar. 19-31/5/55.**N/C.**
Dar. 9-14/5/57.**N/C.**

BOILERS:
  2124.
  2125 *(ex336)* 22/12/34.
  2023 *(ex277)* 28/9/36.
  2592 *(ex366)* 14/6/41.
  2600 *(ex283)* 11/3/44.
  3976 *(new)* 17/6/49.
  27392 *(ex2751)* 6/2/52.
  27422 *(ex2749)* 25/4/53.
  27359 *(ex2753)* 26/2/55.

SHEDS:
York.
Haymarket 16/3/29.
York 8/4/29.
Starbeck 5/10/47.
York 30/5/48.
Scarborough 3/10/53.

RENUMBERED:
  2726 1/12/46.
62726 17/6/49.

CONDEMNED:
18/12/57.

336 BUCKINGHAMSHIRE
THE QUORN (from 9/5/32)

Darlington.

To traffic 1/6/29.

REPAIRS:
Dar. 2/7-16/9/29.**N/C.**
Cow. 30/8/30.**G.**
Dar. 12/3-25/4/31.**N/C.**
Dar. 3/3-9/5/32.**G.** *Re-named.*
Dar. 29/9-28/10/32.**N/C.**
Dar. 11/4-10/7/33.**L.**

Dar. 28/5-29/6/34.**G.**
Dar. 24/7-5/9/36.**G.**
Dar. 26/7-9/8/37.**N/C.**
Heat.Conn.at front.
Dar. 21/6-30/8/38.**G.**
Dar. 11/9-25/10/40.**G.**
Dar. 9/9/42-12/3/43.**G.**
Dar. 1-23/3/44.**L.** *After collision.*
Cow. 3-24/3/45.**G.**
Dar. 12/8-27/9/47.**G.**
Dar. 17/5-19/8/50.**G.**
Dar. 21/8-6/9/50.**N/C.**
Dar. 20/8-13/9/52.**G.**
Dar. 25/6/54-19/2/55.**G.**
Dar. 21/2-12/3/55.**N/C.**
Dar. 12/6-6/7/57.**G.**
Dar. 8-11/7/57.**N/C.**
Dar. 7-17/8/59.**C/L.**

BOILERS:
  2125.
  2044 *(ex322)* 29/6/34.
  2000 *(ex269)* 5/9/36.
  2607 *(ex292)* 25/10/40.
  2014 *(ex357)* 12/3/43.
  1985 *(ex236)* 24/3/45.
  2626 *(ex2734)* 27/9/47.
  27417 *(ex2765)* 13/9/52.
  27363 *(ex2716)* 19/2/55.
  27351 *(ex2710)* 6/7/57.

SHEDS:
York.
Perth 22/11/29.
York 19/2/31.
Hull Botanic Gardens 26/9/38.
Scarborough 15/10/42.
Neville Hill 12/3/45.
Hull Botanic Gardens 19/4/45.
York 8/10/48.
Starbeck 1/10/50.
Hull Dairycoates 13/9/59.

RENUMBERED:
  2727 17/11/46.
62727 19/8/50.

CONDEMNED:
16/1/61.
Cut up at Darlington.

2753 CHESHIRE

Darlington.

To traffic 20/2/29.

REPAIRS:
Dar. 29/4-16/7/31.**G.**
Dar. 31/5-1/7/32.**H.** *New cylinders.*
Dar. 20/6-10/8/33.**G.**
Dar. 15/4-19/7/35.**G.**
Dar. 11/7/36. *Weigh..*

WORKS CODES:- Cow - Cowlairs. Dar - Darlington. Don - Doncaster. Ghd - Gateshead. Gor - Gorton. Inv - Inverurie. Str - Stratford.
REPAIR CODES:- **C/H** - Casual Heavy. **C/L** - Casual Light. **G** - General. **H** - Heavy. **H/I** - Heavy Intermediate. **L** - Light. **L/I** - Light Intermediate. **N/C** - Non-Classified.

24

No.283 THE MIDDLETON was reported as the only D49 to be fitted with speed indicating equipment. When new in August 1933 it had Smith type, but it was soon removed, at a date not recorded, but before it was seen here in Newcastle station on 9th September 1934. *W.B.Greenfield*

The engines built to August 1933, and allocated to North Eastern Area, which were 6 Part 1, 17 Part 2, and 5 Part 3, were fitted with Raven fog signalling apparatus. On this broadside view of no.318 the striker for it can be seen between the rear coupled wheel and the cab footstep. Five Scottish Area engines (264, 270, 309, 329, and 2754) which frequently worked on the East Coast main line into Newcastle, were also reported to have had that apparatus. At the end of October 1933 that warning system went out of use and the equipment was removed from the engines when next they went to works. *J.G.Gregory*

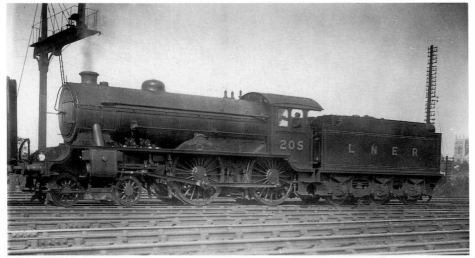

The 25 Part 2 engines built in 1934/35 all worked in the North Eastern Area but were too late for the Raven warning system, so were never equipped for it. The first of that batch no.205 THE ALBRIGHTON here is on station pilot work at York. *WBY collection*

Dar. 29/10-24/12/36.**G.**
Dar. 11/11/37-21/1/38.**L.**
Cow. 17/12/38.**G.**
Cow. 26/8/39.**L.**
Cow. 4/5/40.**G.**
Cow. 21/6/41.**G.** *Hudd A.T.C.fitted.*
Cow. 27/9/41.**L.**
Cow. 7/2/42.**H.**
Cow. 22/5/42.**L.**
Cow. 23/1/43.**G.** *Hudd A.T.C.removed.*
Cow. 7/10/43.**L.**
Cow. 19/5/44.**L.**
Cow. 23/6-7/7/45.**L.**
Cow. 26/1-23/2/46.**G.**
Dar. 21/8-5/10/46.**L.**
Cow. 20-21/12/46.**L.**
Dar. 13-27/9/47.**L.**
Ghd. 30/3-21/4/48.**L.**
Dar. 9/11-23/12/48.**G.**
Dar. 7/12/51-12/1/52.**G.**
Dee. 31/1-23/2/54.**C/L.**
Dee. 6/4-1/7/55.**C/L.**
Dar. 19/12/57-25/1/58.**G.**
Dar. 27-30/1/58.**N/C.**
Dar. 29/10/59. *Not repaired.*

BOILERS:
2164.
2012 (*ex265*) 10/8/33.
2332 (*ex2756*) 24/12/36.
2005 (*ex277*) 4/5/40.
2632 (*ex246*) 7/2/42.
C1798 (*ex2711*) 23/12/48.
27427 (*new*) 12/1/52.
27354 (*2707*) 25/1/58.

SHEDS:
Eastfield.
Perth 23/3/29.
Eastfield 14/7/29.
Dundee 17/4/43.
Perth 2/45.
Dundee 3/45.
Thornton Junction 21/2/57.

RENUMBERED:
2728 7/4/46.
62728 21/4/48.

CONDEMNED:
29/10/59.

2754 RUTLANDSHIRE

Darlington.

To traffic 8/4/29.

REPAIRS:
Cow. 5-7/30.**G.** *New crank axle.*
Dar. 12/11/31-25/1/32.**G.** *Raven F.S.A.fitted. New cylinders.*
Dar. 3/3-21/4/33.**G.**
Dar. 3-4/5/33.**N/C.**
Cow. 29/6/34.**H.**
Dar. 11/7-30/8/35.**G.**
Dar. 2/12/36-23/1/37.**G.**
Dar. 3/2-24/5/38.**G.**
Cow. 4/2/40.**G.**
Cow. 24/5/41.**G.**
Cow. 14/3/42.**L.**
Cow. 19/6/43.**G.**
Cow. 26/10/43.**L.**
Cow. 21/7/45.**L.**
Cow. 13/7/46.**G.**
Dar. 10/7-3/9/48.**G.**
Dar. 5/2-3/3/51.**G.**
Cow. 13-17/11/51.**C/L.**
Dar. 28/8-26/9/53.**G.**
Dar. 28-29/9/53.**N/C.**
Dar. 23/9-22/10/55.**G.**
Dar. 29/10-30/11/57.**H/I.**

BOILERS:
2174.
2046 (*ex329*) 21/4/33.
1986 (*ex265*) 30/8/35.
2012 (*ex2753*) 23/1/37.
2038 (*exDARL.&366*) 4/2/40.
2592 (*ex352*) 13/7/46.
2765 (*ex362*) 3/9/48.
27364 (*ex2775*) 3/3/51.

27370 (*ex2722*) 26/9/53.
27438 (*new*) 22/10/55.

SHEDS:
Eastfield.
Haymarket 26/7/29.
Carlisle 12/33.
Thornton Junction 29/12/47.
St Margarets 9/4/60.

RENUMBERED:
2729 13/7/46.
62729 3/9/48.

CONDEMNED:
1/5/61.
Cut up at Darlington.

2755 BERKSHIRE

Darlington.

To traffic 15/3/29.

REPAIRS:
Cow. 19-20/3/29.**N/C.**
Dar. 28/2-16/5/31.**G.**
Dar. 6/3-4/5/33.**G.** *New cylinders.*
Dar. 29/9-11/10/33.**N/C.**
Dar. 13/10-2/12/33.**N/C.**
Dar. 3/10-24/11/34.**G.**
Dar. 28/11/35-29/1/36.**G.**
Dar. 13-31/3/36.**N/C.**
Dar. 12/11/36-16/1/37.**G.**
Dar. 13-21/5/37.**N/C.**
Dar. 5/10-2/12/37.**G.**
Cow. 24-28/4/39.**N/C.**
Cow. 26/8-16/10/39.**G.**
Cow. 25/11/41. *Sent to Darlington.*
Dar. 1/12/41-19/1/42.**G.**
Cow. 5-9/11/42.**L.**
Cow. 6-8/5/43.**L.**
Cow. 3-18/10/43.**L.**
Cow. 15-21/7/44.**H.**
Cow. 2-20/9/44.**G.**
Cow. 21/7-4/8/45.**L.**
Cow. 12/11-1/12/45.**L.**

Dar. 5/11/46-16/1/47.**G.**
Dar. 26/9-10/11/47.**L.**
Dar. 1/4-6/5/49.**G.**
Dar. 27/6-16/8/52.**L/I.**
Dar. 27/10-14/12/54.**G.**
Dar. 21/12/54-7/1/55.**N/C.**
Dar. 11/12/58. *Not repaired.*

BOILERS:
2148.
2174 (*ex2754*) 4/5/33.
2124 (*ex352*) 24/11/34.
7951 (*ex235*) 29/1/36.
2615 (*ex370*) 19/1/42.
7947 (*ex318*) 20/9/44.
2041 (*ex374*) 16/1/47.
3963 (*new*) 6/5/49.
3963 Ren. 27419 16/8/52.
27415 (*ex2708*) 14/12/54.

SHEDS:
Eastfield.
Carlisle 4/5/36.
Starbeck 17/9/50.
York 1/10/50.
Selby 17/8/58.

RENUMBERED:
2730 2/6/46.
62730 19/9/48.

CONDEMNED:
11/12/58.

2756 SELKIRKSHIRE

Darlington.

To traffic 21/3/29.

REPAIRS:
Cow. 25-26/3/29.**N/C.**
Dar. 20/5-23/6/31.**G.**
Dar. 18/5-14/7/33.**G.**
Cow. 20-26/12/33.**L.**
Dar. 21/12/34-11/2/35.**G.**
Dar. 24/4-29/5/35.**L.**

Cow. 25-31/12/35.**L.**
Dar. 18/9-21/11/36.**G.**
Cow. 30/6-5/7/37.**L.**
Cow. 30/8-11/9/37.**L.**
Dar. 24/3-5/8/38. *Not repaired.*
Cow. 16/8-19/9/38.**G.**
Cow. 29/9-11/10/38.**L.**
Cow. 7-9/3/39.**L.**
Cow. 31/5-5/6/39.**L.**
Cow. 23-28/6/39.**L.**
Cow. 24/3-8/5/41.**G.**
Cow. 4-24/11/41.**L.**
Cow. 20/1-23/2/44.**H.**
Cow. 8-21/3/45.**L.**
Cow. 25/6-11/7/45.**H.**
Cow. 16/4-17/5/46.**G.**
Dar. 20/8-10/10/47.**L.**
Dar. 18/10-26/11/48.**G.**
Dar. 17-29/12/48.**C/L.**
Dar. 6/9-1/10/49.**C/L.**
Ghd. 23/11-18/12/50.**C/L.**
Dar. 18/3-10/4/52.**G.**
Ghd. 4/8-24/9/54.**C/L.**
Ghd. 14/10-12/11/54.**C/H.**
Ghd. 5/6-6/7/56.**G.**
Ghd. 9-13/7/56.**N/C.**
Dar. 3/4/59. *Not repaired.*

BOILERS:
2151.
2332 *(ex245)* 11/2/35.
2616 *(ex368)* 21/11/36.
2009 (C1657) *(ex2759)* 8/5/41.
2005 (C1658) *(ex250)* 11/7/45.
2592 *(ex2729)* 26/11/48.
27404 *(ex2736)* 10/4/52.
27378 *(ex2719)* 6/7/56.

SHEDS:
Eastfield.
Carlisle 1/3/37.
Starbeck 17/9/50.
York 1/10/50.
Scarborough 6/7/52.
Pickering 14/9/52.
York 1/2/53.
Starbeck 20/2/55.
York 26/6/55.
Selby 16/6/57.

RENUMBERED:
2731 2/6/46.
62731 19/9/48.

CONDEMNED:
3/4/59.

2757 DUMFRIES-SHIRE

Darlington.

To traffic 28/3/29.

REPAIRS:
Dar. 29/5-20/8/31.**G.** *New crank axle.*

Designed in Darlington drawing office, it was only to be expected that the top lamp iron would be their pattern and mounted on top of the smokebox. That item was only disturbed after they went to Cowlairs works for maintenance. 264 is climbing Cowlairs incline on an express out of Glasgow (Queen St). *WBY collection*

Between Edinburgh and Perth, the latter's portion of the Flying Scotsman train was often to be seen carrying its headboard. This view of 250 PERTHSHIRE at Perth shed clearly shows how ridiculous, even dangerous, it was when mounted on a lamp iron above the smokebox. *T.G.Hepburn*

Dar. 18/4-15/6/33.**G.** *New cylinders.*
Dar. 11/10-10/12/34.**G.**
Dar. 12/8-27/9/35.**L.**
Dar. 18/2-10/3/36.**L.**
Dar. 19/8-8/10/36.**G.**
Dar. 18/1-23/5/38.**G.**
Cow. 12/6/39.**L.**
Cow. 11/11/39.**G.**
Cow. 12/10/40.**L.**
Cow. 20/9/41.**G.**
Cow. 10/3/44.**G.**
Cow. 9-16/6/45.**L.**
Cow. 1-8/9/45.**L.**
Dar. 1/11/46-31/5/47.**G.**

Dar. 28/12/48-18/2/49.**G.**
Dar. 23-25/2/49.**N/C.**
Dar. 16/5-14/6/52.**H/I.**
Dar. 16-26/6/52.**N/C.**
Dar. 7-13/1/54.**N/C.**
Dar. 24/5-19/6/54.**G.**
Dar. 21-23/6/54.**N/C.**
Dar. 1-2/7/54.**N/C.**
Car. 9/8-22/9/55.**C/L.**
Dar. 27/6-15/8/56.**G.**
Dar. 11/9/58. *Not repaired.*

BOILERS:
2154.
2174 *(ex2755)* 10/12/34.

2605 *(ex357)* 8/10/36.
2051 *(ex2758)* 20/9/41.
3783 *(new)* 31/5/47.
3783 Ren. 27414 14/6/52.
27411 *(ex2734)* 19/6/54.
27357 *(ex2704)* 15/8/56.

SHEDS:
Eastfield.
Carlisle 1/3/37.
Starbeck 17/9/50.
York 1/10/50.
Carlisle 15/7/51.
Darlington 2/11/58.

In Scottish Area it was common for a curved destination board to be carried, in a pair of clips on the rim of the smokebox, as here on an Aberdeen to Glasgow train approaching Cupar. Use of those boards prevented a lamp being carried on the top iron, so in the early 1930's, Cowlairs began to replace the Darlington style by one of Group Standard pattern fixed on the smokebox door just above the upper hinge strap. 2759 has been so altered, and carried lamp to indicate a stopping passenger train, without any interference with the Glasgow destination board. *T.G.Hepburn*

Some destination boards were fitted with a clip on their face, which enabled them to be carried on the door lamp iron when that was not needed to indicate type of train. On 19th June 1936 Carlisle's 2754 worked an express on the Waverley Route, so was able to carry the Edinburgh destination board on the door lamp iron. *W.A.Camwell*

Despite the effort by Cowlairs to put the top lamp iron lower, and so more easily accessible, by nationalisation Darlington custom had prevailed, and all seen thereafter had iron in original position above the smokebox. 62711 worked the whole of its life from the two Edinburgh sheds, and as no.281 in the 1930's, did have lamp moved down on to the door. As seen here at St Margarets shed in August 1960 it had reverted, but then had one of Group Standard pattern. Note that it had been fitted for slipping the front coupling so that it could be used for banking expresses up to Cockburnspath on the East Coast main line, a sad decline from being built to haul, not just to push them. *P.H.Groom*

All the 76 engines originally had the full plate covering the gap, hinged on the tender to ride free on the engine. Experience showed that arrangement could lead to occasional cases of a fireman having a foot trapped. *W.Potter*

From about 1940 the hazard of trapped feet was reduced by hinging the fall plate on the engine, so as to ride free on the tender. That put the danger area further to the rear, and all were then so changed, irrespective of the type of tender with which they were coupled. Note this ex Great Central tender has changed to Group Standard buffers. *I.H.B.Lewis*

Starting in 1935, Darlington added train heating hose connection under the front buffer beam to the 71 engines not so fitted hitherto. No.247 THE BLANKNEY was so equipped when ex works from this general repair. *C.L.Turner*

For working between Dundee and Aberdeen, which included a short length of single track near Montrose, eight of the first D49s allocated to Scottish Area were fitted with tablet exchanging apparatus. That avoided them having to slow to a crawl for hand exchange when working expresses, as 310 was about to do from Dundee on 8th June 1936. *W.A.Camwell*

2757 continued.
RENUMBERED:
2732 12/4/46.
62732 19/9/48.

CONDEMNED:
3/11/58.

2758 NORTHUMBERLAND

Darlington.

To traffic 28/3/29.

REPAIRS:
Cow. 4/31. *After derailment.*
Dar. 9/12/31-18/1/32.**L.**
Dar. 3-17/11/32. *Tender only.*
Cow. 15/5-22/6/34.**G.**
Dar. 16/11/34-30/1/35.**L.**
Dar. 1/11-27/12/35.**G.** *New cyls.*
Dar. 1/6-14/7/36.**L.**
Dar. 4/12/36-9/2/37.**G.**
Cow. 23/9/38.**N/C.**
Cow. 10/6/39.**N/C.** *Hudd.A.T.C. fitted.*
Cow. 22/12/39.**L.**
Cow. 20/7/40.**G.**
Cow. 12/7/41.**G.**
Cow. 12/2/42.**L.**
Cow. 9/4/42.**L.**
Cow. 13/2/43.**G.** *Hudd A.T.C.removed.*
Cow. 21/6/43.**L.**
Cow. 27/6/44.**H.**
Cow. 21/9/44.**L.**
Cow. 13/1/45.**H.**
Cow. 14/12/45.**L.**
Cow. 27/7/46.**H.**
Dar. 25/4-7/6/47.**L.**
Dar. 11-31/3/48.**L.**
Dar. 28/12/48-15/2/49.**G.**
Dar. 3/4-5/5/51.**G.**
Ghd. 9-10/5/51.**N/C.**
Ghd. 18/9-8/10/52.**C/L.**
Dar. 17/11/53-24/2/54.**G.**
StRx 4-29/5/54.**N/C.**
Cow. 12-13/8/55.**N/C.**
Dar. 18/2-22/3/57.**G.**
Dar. 23-29/10/58.**C/L.**
Cow. 4-5/10/60.**N/C.**

BOILERS:
2160.
2051 *(ex335)* 9/2/37.
1983 *(ex249)* 12/7/41.
2615 *(ex2755)* 13/1/45.
2701 *(ex2951)* 15/2/49.
2701 Renumbered 27375 5/5/51.
27419 *(ex2722)* 22/3/57.

SHEDS:
Eastfield.
St Margarets 6/29.
Eastfield 1/33.
Haymarket 8/43.

Thornton Junction 27/1/58.
St Margarets 18/4/60.
Hawick 16/1/61.

RENUMBERED:
2733 1/12/46.
62733 31/3/48.

CONDEMNED:
24/4/61.
Cut up at Darlington.

2759 CUMBERLAND

Darlington.

To traffic 31/5/29.

REPAIRS:
Dar. 9/10-1/12/33.**G.** *New cylinders.*
Dar. 8/5-25/6/35.**G.**
Dar. 6/5-7/7/36.**L.**
Dar. 30/10-23/12/36.**G.**
Dar. 1/11/37-19/1/38.**G.** *New frames.*
Cow. 18/2/39.**L.**
Cow. 17/2/40.**G.**
Cow. 19/4/41.**G.** *Hudd A.T.C.fitted.*
Cow. 31/7/41.**L.**
Cow. 19/9/42.**G.** *Hudd A.T.C.removed.*
Cow. 17/9/43.**L.**
Cow. 3/11/44.**G.**
Cow. 29/9/45.**G.**
Cow. 18/5/46.**L.**
Dar. 15/7-12/9/47.**G.**
Ghd. 15/11-3/12/48.**L.**
Dar. 9/11-9/12/49.**G.**
Dar. 19/2-9/3/51.**C/L.**
Ghd. 14/11-5/12/51.**C/L.**
Dar. 5-30/8/52.**G.**
Dar. 1-4/9/52.**N/C.**
Ghd. 29/5-29/6/53.**C/L.**
Dar. 30/3-8/5/54.**G.**
Dar. 11-14/5/54.**N/C.**
Dar. 24/4-1/6/56.**G.**
Dar. 4/3/61. *Not repaired.*

BOILERS:
2163.
2009 (C1657)*(ex306)* 23/12/36.
7949 *(ex281)* 19/4/41.
2626 *(ex274)* 29/9/45.
3784 *(new)* 12/9/47.
2014 *(ex2735)* 9/12/49.
27411 *(ex2731)* 30/8/52.
27373 *(ex2715)* 8/5/54.
27390 *(ex2721)* 1/6/56.

SHEDS:
Eastfield.
Haymarket 8/43.
Carlisle 2/12/46.
Starbeck 17/9/50.

York 1/10/50.
Carlisle 15/7/51.

RENUMBERED:
2734 17/11/46.
62734 19/9/48.

CONDEMNED:
4/3/61.

2760 WESTMORLAND

Darlington.

To traffic 20/6/29.

REPAIRS:
Dar. 27/7-22/9/31.**G.**
Dar. 18/1-1/4/33.**G.**
Cow. 31/7-10/10/34.**L.**
Dar. 14/10-31/12/35.**G.**
Cow. 26/8-14/10/36.**H.**
Dar. 22/10-3/11/36.**L.**
Dar. 25/11/37-27/1/38.**L.**
Cow. 7/10-25/11/38.**G.**
Cow. 9-26/5/39.**L.**
Cow. 21/11-12/12/39.**L.**
Cow. 11-14/6/40.**N/C.**
Cow. 24/9-14/10/40.**G.**
Cow. 26/11-13/12/40.**N/C.** *Hudd A.T.C. fitted.*
Cow. 9/6-4/7/41.**L.**
Cow. 13-18/7/41.**N/C.**
Cow. 26/3-1/5/42.**G.** *Hudd A.T.C. removed.*
Cow. 8-11/6/42.**N/C.**
Cow. 23-25/6/42.**N/C.**
Cow. 27/10-21/11/42.**L.**
Cow. 29/3-10/4/43.**L.**
Cow. 8/5-4/6/43.**L.**
Cow. 24/8-24/9/43.**G.**
Cow. 29/10-23/11/44.**L.**
Cow. 23/4-5/5/45.**L.**
Cow. 9/7-17/8/45.**G.**
Cow. 12/11-21/12/45.**L.**
Cow. 3/5-8/6/46.**L.**
Dar. 15/7-3/10/47.**G.**
Dar. 20/10-5/11/47.**N/C.**
Dar. 9/8-2/9/49.**G.**
Dar. 17/7-28/8/52.**H/I.**
Dar. 4/6-7/7/54.**G.**
Dar. 25/8/58. *Not repaired.*

BOILERS:
2171.
2148 *(ex311)* 14/10/40.
2014 *(ex336)* 17/8/45.
3993 *(new)* 2/9/49.
3993 Ren. 27420 28/8/52.
27416 *(ex2713)* 7/7/54.

SHEDS:
Eastfield.
Haymarket 8/43.
Carlisle 2/12/46.
Starbeck 17/9/50.

York 1/10/50.
Scarborough 11/4/54.

RENUMBERED:
2735 17/11/46.
62735 19/9/48.

CONDEMNED:
25/8/58.

201 THE BRAMHAM MOOR

Darlington.

To traffic 20/4/32.

REPAIRS:
Dar. 15/9-4/11/33.**G.**
Dar. 28/11/33-7/2/34.**L.**
Dar. 11/5-6/6/34.**L.**
Dar. 10/9-31/10/35.**G.**
Dar. 27/4-10/6/37.**G.**
Dar. 29/10-28/11/38.**L.**
Dar. 22/2-13/4/39.**G.**
Dar. 4-26/6/40.**L.**
Dar. 11/3-15/4/41.**G.**
Dar. 19-23/4/41.**N/C.**
Dar. 17-29/9/41.**N/C.**
Cow. 17/9/42.**L.**
Dar. 7/10/42-30/1/43.**G.** *New frames. Goodall drawbar off.*
Cow. 5-24/2/45.**G.**
Dar. 23/12/47-13/2/48.**G.**
Dar. 4/9-4/10/50.**G.**
Dar. 10/2-7/3/53.**H/I.**
Dar. 9-11/3/53.**N/C.**
Dar. 4-11/8/54.**C/L.**
Dar. 30/9-29/10/55.**G.**
Dar. 31/10-1/11/55.**N/C.**

BOILERS:
C7947.
1985 *(ex309)* 31/10/35.
7950 *(ex266)* 10/6/37.
2002 *(ex362)* 15/4/41.
1990 *(ex211)* 24/2/45.
2950 *(ex2710)* 13/2/48.
27351 *(ex2757)* 4/10/50.
27425 *(ex2739)* 29/10/55.

SHEDS:
Neville Hill.
Gateshead 18/12/34.
York 8/10/48.
Starbeck 1/10/50.
Neville Hill 16/6/57.
Starbeck 23/6/57.

RENUMBERED:
2736 14/4/46.
E2736 13/2/48.
62736 4/10/51.

CONDEMNED:
19/6/58.

211 THE YORK AND AINSTY

Darlington.

To traffic 4/5/32.

REPAIRS:
Dar. 25/8-7/9/32.**N/C.**
Dar. 1/12/33-16/2/34.**G.**
Dar. 5-20/11/34.**N/C.**
Dar. 20/9-8/11/35.**G.**
Dar. 23/2-6/4/37.**G.**
Dar. 9-17/6/37.**N/C.** *Heat.conn.at front.*
Dar. 23/1-10/3/39.**G.**
Dar. 14-28/9/40.**L.**
Dar. 6/10-19/11/41.**G.** *Goodall drawbar off.*
Dar. 30/9-6/10/42.**L.**
Dar. 21/5-8/6/43.**L.**
Cow. 16/5-8/7/44.**G.**
Cow. 17/11/45-19/1/46.**G.**
Cow. 2/3-6/4/46.**L.**
Dar. 12/10-9/11/46.**L.**
Ghd. 9-19/4/47.**L.**
Dar. 9/4-4/5/48.**L.**
Dar. 5/11-15/12/48.**G.**
Dar. 23/12/48-5/1/49.**N/C.**
Ghd. 21/3-21/4/50.**L/I.**
Dar. 9/11-14/12/51.**G.**
Dar. 5/12/53-16/1/54.**G.**
Dar. 25-26/1/54.**N/C.**
Dar. 11/8-27/9/55.**G.**
Dar. 10-13/7/56.**C/L.**
Dar. 10/1-13/2/57.**G.**
Dar. 5-13/3/57.**N/C.**
Dar. 11/12/57. *Not repaired.*

BOILERS:
C7948.
2019 *(ex266)* 8/11/35.
2017 *(ex310)* 6/4/37.
2044 *(ex226)* 10/3/39.
1990 *(ex230)* 19/11/41.
2614 *(ex217)* 8/7/44.
3173 *(ex2744)* 15/12/48.
27393 *(ex2763)* 14/12/51.
27426 *(ex2717)* 26/1/54.
27387 *(ex2741)* 27/9/55.
27403 *(ex2759)* 13/2/57.

SHEDS:
Neville Hill.
Gateshead 13/12/34.
Alston 27/5/40.
Tweedmouth 2/11/40.
Neville Hill 23/7/45.
Hull Botanic Gardens 12/5/46.

RENUMBERED:
2737 28/4/46.
62737 4/5/48.

CONDEMNED:
1/1/58.

220 THE ZETLAND

Darlington.

To traffic 3/5/32.

REPAIRS:
Dar. 7/9-24/10/33.**G.**
Dar. 26/3-9/5/34.**H.**
Dar. 30/7-13/9/35.**G.**
Dar. 16/8-29/9/37.**G.** *Heat.conn.at front.*
Dar. 26/7-1/9/39.**G.**
Dar. 6/8-20/9/41.**G.** *Goodall drawbar off.*
Dar. 8/6-30/7/42.**L/I.**
Dar. 2-9/11/42.**N/C.**
Dar. 30/1-13/3/43.**L.**
Cow. 24/5-24/6/44.**G.**
Cow. 16/6-14/7/45.**H.** *Rear sanding fitted.*
Cow. 13/10-3/11/45.**L.**
Cow. 27/7-7/9/46.**L.**
Ghd. 28/1-7/2/47.**L.**
Dar. 16/6-9/8/47.**G.**
Dar. 12-22/8/47.**N/C.**
Ghd. 25/6-19/7/48.**L/I.**
Ghd. 1-11/2/49.**L/I.**
Dar. 14/12/49-28/1/50.**G.**
Ghd. 3-9/2/50.**N/C.**
Dar. 17/2-8/3/50.**N/C.**
Dar. 13-22/12/51.**C/L.**
Dar. 8/2-16/5/52.**G.** *New frames & mod.bogie.*
Dar. 1/9/54-22/4/55.**H/I.**
Dar. 16/8-14/9/57.**G.**
Dar. 16-17/9/57.**N/C.**

BOILERS:
C7949.
2654 *(new)* 13/9/35.
7966 *(ex283)* 1/9/39.
124 *(ex238)* 20/9/41.
3799 *(new)* 9/8/47.
2596 *(ex2770)* 28/1/50.
27428 *(new)* 16/5/52.
27389 *(ex2760)* 14/9/57.

SHEDS:
Neville Hill.
Gateshead 26/1/35.
Hull Botanic Gardens 13/7/36.
Gateshead 2/1/41.
Starbeck 26/9/48.
York 13/9/59.

RENUMBERED:
2738 19/5/46.
62738 11/2/49.

CONDEMNED:
21/9/59.

232 THE BADSWORTH

Darlington.

To traffic 17/5/32.

REPAIRS:
Dar. 17/1-23/2/34.**G.**
Dar. 17/5-15/6/34.**L.**
Dar. 24/3-29/7/36.**G.**
Dar. 30/7-19/8/36.**N/C.**
Dar. 4/4-3/6/38.**G.**
Dar. 6/2-12/3/40.**G.**
Dar. 18/6-11/7/40.**L.**
Dar. 3/7-8/8/41.**L.**
Dar. 29/6-8/8/42.**G.** *Goodall drawbar off.*
Dar. 18/12/42-27/1/43.**L.**
Cow. 1/7-5/8/44.**G.**
Cow. 23/6-14/7/45.**L.**
Dar. 13/8-7/9/46.**L.**
Dar. 9/6-23/8/47.**G.**
Dar. 31/12/49-10/2/50.**G.**
Dar. 25/10-24/11/51.**G.**
Dar. 27/8-7/10/53.**C/H.**
Dar. 26/7-18/11/55.**G.**
Dar. 3/4-8/5/58.**G.**
Dar. 11/10/60. *Not repaired.*

BOILERS:
C7950.
1996 *(ex251)* 23/2/34.
2611 *(ex363)* 29/7/36.
2613 *(ex269)* 12/3/40.
2634 *(ex359)* 8/8/42.
3786 *(ex2716)* 10/2/50.
27425 *(new)* 24/11/51.
27423 *(ex2764)* 18/11/55.
27409 *(ex2740)* 8/5/58.

SHEDS:
York.
Gateshead 28/8/36.
Neville Hill 15/8/48.
Scarborough 1/7/51.

RENUMBERED:
2739 14/4/46.
62739 10/2/50.

CONDEMNED:
11/10/60.

235 THE BEDALE

Darlington.

To traffic 2/6/32.

REPAIRS:
Dar. 9/6-7/7/33.**L.**
Dar. 1/12/33-25/1/34.**G.**
Dar. 4/11/35-21/1/36.**G.**
Dar. 22/8-3/10/38.**G.** *Heater conn.at front.*
Dar. 15/6-1/8/39.**H.**

Dar. 31/7-7/8/40.**N/C.**
Dar. 29/4-20/6/41.**G.** *Goodall drawbar off.*
Dar. 26/6-8/8/42.**L/I.**
Dar. 7-19/9/42.**L.**
Cow. 16/10-4/11/43.**G.**
Dar. 21/3-12/4/44.**L.**
Cow. 3/11-2/12/44.**L.**
Cow. 27/10-1/12/45.**G.**
Cow. 11-29/12/45.**N/C.**
Orig.boiler re-fitted.
Dar. 1/5-12/7/47.**G.**
Dar. 25/10-2/12/49.**G.**
Dar. 28/2-27/3/52.**H/I.**
Dar. 7-30/5/53.**C/L.**
Dar. 9/4-22/9/54.**G.**
Dar. 7/12/56-7/1/57.**C/H.**
Dar. 27/8-28/9/57.**G.**
Dar. 30/9-2/10/57.**N/C.**
Dar. 21/7/60. *Not repaired.*

BOILERS:
C7951.
2041 *(ex247)* 21/1/36.
2765 *(ex282)* 20/6/41.
7948 *(ex307)* 4/11/43.
2952 *(ex245)* 1/12/45.
7948 *(ex spare)* 29/12/45 re-fitted.
2603 *(ex2701)* 12/7/47.
4003 *(new)* 2/12/49.
4003 Renumbered 27409 27/3/52.
25807 *(ex4712)* 28/9/57.

SHEDS:
York.
Starbeck 1/10/50.
Neville Hill 8/7/56.
York 30/11/58.
Selby 14/6/59.
Hull Dairycoates 13/9/59.

RENUMBERED:
2740 28/4/46.
62740 2/12/49.

CONDEMNED:
1/8/60.

247 THE BLANKNEY

Darlington.

To traffic 14/7/32.

REPAIRS:
Dar. 26/2-29/3/34.**G.**
Dar. 23/9-14/11/35.**G.**
Dar. 14/9-25/10/37.**G.** *Heat.conn.at front.*
Dar. 12/7-23/8/39.**G.**
Dar. 25/4-30/5/42.**G.** *Goodall drawbar off.*
Dar. 6-19/10/42.**N/C.**
Cow. 12/5-24/6/44.**G.**

By 1931, Pacifics had taken over the faster trains on the Aberdeen-Dundee line, so tablet exchanger was no longer needed on D49 class. When Cowlairs removed them, they plugged the resultant hole in the side of the cab, through which it had been operated. Most, but not all, duly lost that hole in the cab side, but it could still be seen on **62713 ABERDEENSHIRE** when at Darlington on 14th August 1957, at a visit which resulted in it being withdrawn. Incidentally, that hole can still be observed on the preserved D49 class 246 **MORAYSHIRE**. *R.A.Panting*

Cow. 19-28/10/44.**L.**
Cow. 20/10-10/11/45.**G.**
Ghd. 28/2-20/3/47.**L.**
Dar. 10/6-23/8/49.**G.**
Dar. 24/9-20/10/51.**G.**
Dar. 29/5-24/10/53.**G.**
Dar. 26/10-6/11/53.**N/C.**
Dar. 13/7-13/8/55.**G.**
Dar. 1-31/5/57.**G.**

BOILERS:
C7952.
 2041 *(ex236)* 29/3/34.
 7947 *(ex201)* 14/11/35.
 2034 *(ex288)* 25/10/37.
 2017 *(ex211)* 23/8/39.
 2151 *(ex245)* 30/5/42.
 7966 *(ex288)* 24/6/44.
 3979 *(new)* 23/8/49.
 27387 *(ex2710)* 20/10/51.
 27360 *(ex2711)* 13/8/55.
 27426 *(ex2720)* 31/5/57.

SHEDS:
York.
Gateshead 23/11/40.
Hull Botanic Gardens 12/5/46.

RENUMBERED:
 2741 8/9/46.
 62741 23/8/49.

CONDEMNED:
30/10/58.

255 THE BRAES OF DERWENT

Darlington.

To traffic 3/8/32.

REPAIRS:
Dar. 15/3-20/4/34.**G.**
Dar. 24/10-17/12/35.**G.**
Dar. 28/8-17/9/36.**L.**
Dar. 16/12/36-5/2/37.**L.**
Dar. 20/4-20/5/37.**L.**
Dar. 25/4-11/6/38.**G.** *Heat.Conn.at front.*
Dar. 15/3-10/4/40.**L.**
Dar. 27/11/40-1/1/41.**G.**
Dar. 12/4-17/5/43.**G.** *Goodall drawbar off.*
Cow. 8-26/8/44.**L.**
Dar. 27/12/44-15/2/45.**L.** *After derailment.*
Cow. 17/11-29/12/45.**G.**
Dar. 11/7-1/9/49.**L.**
Dar. 28/9/50-3/2/51.**G.** *Bogie rebuilt and manganese liners to boxes.*
Dar. 5-6/2/51.**N/C.**

Dar. 6/3-25/4/53.**H/I.**
Dar. 27/4-5/5/53.**N/C.**
Dar. 4-12/6/53.**N/C.**
Dar. 17/6-13/7/53.**N/C.**
Dar. 12/7-11/8/55.**G.**
Dar. 13-26/9/55.**N/C.**
Dar. 12/11/58. *Not repaired:*

BOILERS:
C7953.
 7952 *(ex247)* 20/4/34.
 2626 *(ex357)* 11/6/38.
  127 *(ex375)* 1/1/41.
 2711 *(ex1534)* 17/5/43.
 2711 Renumbered 27365 3/2/51.
 27369 *(ex2700)* 11/8/55.

SHEDS:
York.
Whitby 1/7/39.
York 11/9/39.
Gateshead 29/9/46.
York 7/11/48.
Neville Hill 1/10/50.

RENUMBERED:
 2742 27/10/46.
 62742 1/9/49.

CONDEMNED:
12/11/58.

269 THE CLEVELAND

Darlington.

To traffic 23/8/32.

REPAIRS:
Dar. 17/4-19/5/34.**G.**
Dar. 25/5-28/6/34.**N/C.** *Modified camshaft fitted.*
Dar. 30/4-13/6/36.**G.**
Dar. 21/4-11/6/38.**G.**
Dar. 26/1-2/3/40.**G.**
Dar. 3-12/7/41.**N/C.**
Dar. 21/8-23/9/42.**G.** *Goodall drawbar off.*
Cow. 3-27/5/44.**G.**
Dar. 10-27/11/44.**L.**
Cow. 5-19/5/45.**L.**
Cow. 29/12/45-9/2/46.**G.**
Dar. 14/9-15/10/48.**G.**
Dar. 24/8-15/12/50.**G.** *Bogie rebuilt and manganese liners to coupled boxes.*
Hay. 19/10-12/11/53.**C/L.**
Dar. 19/5-30/12/54.**G.**
Dar. 28/8-10/9/58.**C/L.**
Dar. 14/4/60. *Not repaired.*

BOILERS:
C7954.
 2000 *(ex256)* 19/5/34.

The Part 2 engines all had, and retained, two 8-feed mechanical lubricators for the cylinders and valves; they were mounted side by side on the left-hand running plate. To be frank - I have found no evidence to justify any claim that the naming of 238 as THE BURTON was for the most dedicated LNER enthusiast it has been my delight to meet, or for his Father who, for forty years kept Cottingham in the top bracket for Best Station Garden award in North Eastern Area. *53A Models (Hull) collection*

Between August 1949 and May 1952, five, 62738/41/42/43/44 had their solid bronze axleboxes changed to cast steel with manganese steel liners to their horn cheeks. To serve the new axleboxes, an additional Wakefield 4-feed mechanical lubricator was added. It too was on the left-hand running plate as seen on 62743 THE CLEVELAND at Haymarket shed on 1st September 1957. *P.H.Groom*

2613 *(ex364)* 13/6/36.
2614 *(ex273)* 2/3/40.
2017 *(ex247)* 23/9/42.
2602 *(ex2705)* 15/10/48.
2602 Ren. 27355 15/12/50.
27401 *(ex2760)* 30/12/54.

SHEDS:
York.
Bridlington 9/5/38.
Hull Botanic Gardens 11/7/38.
York 26/9/38.
Gateshead 22/11/40.
Hull Botanic Gardens 12/5/46.
Haymarket 1/1/51.

RENUMBERED:
2743 17/11/46.
62743 15/10/48.

CONDEMNED:
9/5/60.

273 THE HOLDERNESS

Darlington.

To traffic 12/10/32.

REPAIRS:
Dar. 7/2-22/3/34.**G.**
Dar. 27/3-5/7/35.**G.** *New middle cylinder.*
Dar. 28/9-11/12/36.**G.**
Dar. 14/2-8/4/38.**G.** *Heat.conn.at front.*
Dar. 10/10-17/11/39.**G.**
Dar. 12-27/2/40.**N/C.**
Dar. 23/7-12/8/40.**N/C.**
Dar. 14/10-21/11/40.**L.**
Dar. 14/1-17/2/42.**G.** *Goodall drawbar off.*
Dar. 8/9-17/10/42.**L.** *After collision.*
Dar. 27/10-20/11/43.**L.**
Cow. 12/10-4/11/44.**G.**

Dar. 24/8-7/11/46.**G.**
Dar. 15-22/11/46.**N/C.**
Ghd. 15/8-3/9/47.**L.**
Dar. 3/9-15/10/48.**G.**
Dar. 17/9-20/10/51.**G.** *Mod.bogie & manganese liners to coupled boxes.*
Dar. 22-23/10/51.**N/C.**
Dar. 19/2-25/3/54.**G.**
Ghd. 20/9-2/11/56.**G.**
Cow. 30/12/60. *Not repaired.*

BOILERS:
C7955.
Renumbered 7965 5/7/35.
2614 *(ex365)* 11/12/36.
2034 *(ex247)* 17/11/39.
2024 *(ex288)* 17/2/42.
2953 *(ex357)* 4/11/44.
3173 *(ex1436)* 7/11/46.
2952 *(ex2757)* 15/10/48.
27384 *(ex2774)* 20/10/51.

27410 *(ex2723)* 25/3/54.
27417 *(ex2717)* 2/11/56.

SHEDS:
Neville Hill.
Gateshead 13/12/34.
Hull Botanic Gardens 9/10/45.
York 8/10/48.
Dundee 9/3/52.
Thornton Junction 19/2/57.
Hawick 9/4/60.

RENUMBERED:
2744 15/12/46.
62744 15/10/48.

CONDEMNED:
30/12/60
Cut up at Cowlairs.
tender 20/2/62.
engine 14/3/62.

282 THE HURWORTH

Darlington.

To traffic 24/10/32.

REPAIRS:
Dar. 29/11-6/12/32.**N/C.**
Dar. 9/4-2/7/34.**G.** *Continuous cam off & 7 step cam fitted.*
Dar. 10/12/35-18/2/36.**G.** *Heat.conn.at front.*
Dar. 8/6-3/8/37.**G.**
Dar. 13/1-22/2/39.**G.**
Dar. 24/3-6/5/41.**G.**
Dar. 13-29/10/41.**L.**
Cow. 16/10-6/11/43.**G.**
Cow. 27/12/43-11/1/44.**L.** *Goodall drawbar off.*
Cow. 17/11/45-19/1/46.**G.** *Rear sanding fitted.*
Dar. 10-31/8/46.**L.**
Ghd. 19-30/11/46.**L.**
Dar. 12-14/1/49.Spec. exam
Dar. 8/2-13/5/49.**G.**
Dar. 9/10-10/11/51.**G.**
Dar. 12/3-10/4/54.**G.**
Dar. 12-14/4/54.**N/C.**
Dar. 23-27/4/54.**N/C.**
Dar. 9/5-11/6/56.**G.**
Dar. 16/3/59. *Not repaired.*

BOILERS:
C7956.
 2596 *(ex217)* 18/2/36.
 1985 *(ex201)* 3/8/37.
 2765 *(ex292)* 22/2/39.
 2046 *(ex274)* 6/5/41.
  132 *(ex1448)* 19/1/46.
 2925 *(ex2703)* 13/5/49.
 27389 *(ex2741)* 10/11/51.
 27384 *(ex2744)* 10/4/54.
 27361 *(ex2711)* 11/6/56.

SHEDS:
Neville Hill.
Hull Botanic Gardens 15/5/33.
Neville Hill 2/6/39.
York 5/2/40.
Gateshead 22/11/40.
York 7/11/48.
Starbeck 5/12/54.
York 26/6/55.
Scarborough 17/8/58.

RENUMBERED:
 2745 27/10/46.
 62745 13/5/49.

CONDEMNED:
16/3/59.

283 THE MIDDLETON

Darlington.

To traffic 18/8/33.

REPAIRS:
Dar. 22/5-31/8/35.**G.**
Dar. 20/9-29/10/37.**G.** *Heat.conn.at front.*
Dar. 20/6-8/8/39.**G.**
Dar. 17/6-8/8/41.**G.**
Dar. 30/1-27/2/42.**N/C.**
Dar. 3-19/11/42.**N/C.**
Cow. 8/1-12/2/44.**G.**
Cow. 8/12/45-26/1/46.**G.** *Rear sanding fitted.*
Ghd. 12-28/12/46.**L.**
Dar. 24/3-30/4/48.**L.**
Dar. 6/12/48-5/2/49.**G.**
Dar. 8-15/2/49.**N/C.**
Dar. 7-30/4/49.**C/L.**
Dar. 3/4-3/5/52.**G.**
Dar. 8/10/54-16/7/55.**G.**
Dar. 16/5/58. *Not repaired.*

BOILERS:
1D3177.
Renumbered 124 31/8/35.
 7966 *(ex274)* 29/10/37.
 1985 *(ex282)* 8/8/39.
 2600 *(ex357)* 8/8/41.
 2031 *(ex374)* 12/2/44.
 27399 *(ex2773)* 3/5/52.
 27437 *(new)* 16/7/55.

SHEDS:
York.
Heaton 20/10/33.
Hull Botanic Gardens 31/8/35.
Neville Hill 8/6/39.
Scarborough 15/5/48.
Neville Hill 29/5/48.
York 22/7/51.
Starbeck 23/11/52.

RENUMBERED:
 2746 10/11/46.
 62746 30/4/48.

CONDEMNED:
16/5/58.

288 THE PERCY

Darlington.

To traffic 21/8/33.

REPAIRS:
Dar. 31/1-14/3/35.**G.**
Dar. 26/5-10/7/37.**G.** *Heat.conn.at front.*

Dar. 29/12/38-10/2/39.**G.**
Dar. 27/9-5/11/41.**G.**
Cow. 14/4-27/5/44.**G.**
Cow. 24/11/45-12/1/46.**G.**
Ghd. 29/12/46-15/1/47.**L.**
Dar. 3-23/4/48.**L.**
Dar. 5/10-12/11/48.**G.**
Ghd. 14/3-5/4/50.**L/I.**
Dar. 23/10-23/11/51.**G.**
Ghd. 27/4-15/5/53.**C/L.**
Dar. 13/10-13/11/53.**G.**
Ghd. 18/7-9/8/55.**C/L.**
Ghd. 14/5-14/6/57.**G.**
Ghd. 17-28/6/57.**N/C.**
Ghd. 12/7-9/8/57.**N/C.**
Dar. 19/9/57-11/1/58.**C/L.** *New cylinders.*
Ghd. 15/8-12/9/58.**C/L.**
Dar. 4/3/61. *Not repaired.*

BOILERS:
2D3177.
 2034 *(ex318)* 14/3/35.
 2002 *(ex250)* 10/7/37.
 2024 *(ex256)* 10/2/39.
 7966 *(ex220)* 5/11/41.
 7950 *(ex205)* 27/5/44.
 7951 *(ex2723)* 12/11/48.
 27391 *(ex2707)* 23/11/51.
 27440 *(ex2727)* 13/11/53.
 27408 *(ex2754)* 14/6/57.

SHEDS:
York.
Gateshead 29/9/46.
Blaydon 2/1/49.
York 10/6/56.
Carlisle 2/11/58.

RENUMBERED:
 2747 8/12/46.
 62747 23/4/48.

CONDEMNED:
4/3/61.

292 THE SOUTHWOLD

Darlington.

To traffic 23/8/33.

REPAIRS:
Dar. 13/3-7/5/35.**G.** *Heat.conn.at front.*
Dar. 23/10-20/11/35.**N/C.** *Prepared for test dept.*
Dar. 14/12/36-9/2/37.**G.**
Dar. 29/10-16/12/38.**G.**
Dar. 14/8-24/9/40.**G.**
Dar. 7/2-14/3/42.**G.** *Goodall drawbar off.*
Dar. 15-26/9/42.**N/C.**

Cow. 8/1-26/2/44.**G.**
Cow. 13/10-10/11/45.**G.**
Dar. 17/10/46-19/2/47.**G.**
Ghd. 24/2-17/3/48.**L.**
Dar. 4/4-9/6/49.**G.**
Dar. 11/7-18/8/51.**G.**
Dar. 20-22/8/51.**N/C.**
Dar. 28/10-26/11/53.**H/I.**
Dar. 8-12/2/54.**N/C.**
Dar. 2-16/3/54.**N/C.**
Dar. 29/10-2/12/55.**G.**

BOILERS:
3D3177.
Renumbered 126 7/5/35.
 2765 *(new)* 9/2/37.
 2607 *(ex361)* 16/12/38.
 7952 *(ex377)* 24/9/40.
 2631 *(ex368)* 14/3/42.
 2777 *(ex226)* 26/2/44.
 3774 *(new)* 19/2/47.
 27377 *(ex2764)* 18/8/51.
 27362 *(ex2751)* 2/12/55.

SHEDS:
Hull Botanic Gardens.
Neville Hill 17/7/39.
York 5/2/40.
Neville Hill 28/2/40.

RENUMBERED:
 2748 12/1/47.
 62748 9/6/49.

CONDEMNED:
17/12/57.

297 THE COTTESMORE

Darlington.

To traffic 30/8/33.

REPAIRS:
Dar. 11/6-21/8/35.**G.**
Dar. 1/3-9/4/37.**G.**
Dar. 8/9-18/10/37.**L.** *Heat.conn.at front.*
Dar. 15/2-6/4/38.**N/C.**
Dar. 26/1-15/3/39.**G.**
Dar. 30/10-3/12/40.**G.**
Dar. 2-20/2/42.**L.**
Dar. 25/11/42-5/1/43.**G.** *Goodall drawbar off.*
Cow. 7/6-15/7/44.**G.**
Cow. 26/1-16/3/46.**G.**
Dar. 11/3-30/4/48.**G.**
Dar. 4/7-12/8/50.**G.**
Dar. 18/11-13/12/52.**G.**
Dar. 15-16/12/52.**N/C.**
Dar. 29/5-29/7/55.**H/I.**
Dar. 2/7/58. *Not repaired.*

WORKS CODES:- Cow - Cowlairs. Dar - Darlington. Don - Doncaster. Ghd - Gateshead. Gor - Gorton. Inv - Inverurie. Str - Stratford.
REPAIR CODES:- **C/H** - Casual Heavy. **C/L** - Casual Light. **G** - General. **H** - Heavy. **H/I** - Heavy Intermediate. **L** - Light. **L/I** - Light Intermediate. **N/C** - Non-Classified.

35

From Cowlairs on 3rd June 1939, no. 329 had been fitted with Hudd Automatic Train Control apparatus, track equipment for which was then being installed between Glasgow and Edinburgh. By July 1941, ten D49 class had been so fitted, but the war put a stop to that scheme, so by February 1943 the Hudd equipment had been taken off those ten. No D49 class engine survived long enough to get British Railways Automatic Warning System. *D.W.Allen*

BOILERS:
4D3177.
Renumbered 127 21/8/35.
  125 *(ex245)* 9/4/37.
  1996 *(ex361)* 3/12/40.
  7965 *(ex214)* 5/1/43.
  2616 *(ex249)* 16/3/46.
  3796 *(new)* 30/4/48.
  3782 *(ex2768)* 12/8/50.
  27353 *(ex2724)* 13/12/52.

SHEDS:
York.
Heaton 25/10/33.
Neville Hill 23/8/35.
York 5/2/40.
Neville Hill 28/2/40.
Gateshead 29/9/46.
Scarborough 15/8/48.
Starbeck 25/9/49.
Neville Hill 27/11/55.

RENUMBERED:
2749 14/7/46.
62749 30/4/48.

CONDEMNED:
2/7/58.

298 THE PYTCHLEY

Darlington.

To traffic 1/9/33.

REPAIRS:
Dar. 8/5-28/6/35.**G.**
Dar. 2-8/7/35.**N/C.**
Dar. 3/6-26/7/37.**G.** *Heat.conn.at front.*

Dar. 27/7-10/8/37.**N/C.**
Dar. 3/11-30/12/38.**N/C.**
Dar. 17/1-27/2/39.**N/C.**
Dar. 17/4-25/5/39.**N/C.**
Dar. 11-19/9/39.**N/C.**
Dar. 26/1-6/3/40.**G.**
Dar. 5-29/12/41. *Tender only.*
Dar. 4/8-9/9/43.**G.** *Goodall drawbar off.*
Cow. 12/1-30/3/46.**G.** *Rear sanding fitted.*
Ghd. 10/6-4/7/47.**L.**
Dar. 27/9-26/10/49.**G.**
Dar. 19/9-12/10/51.**G.**
Dar. 8-19/1/52.**C/L.**
Dar. 9/7-4/6/54.**G.**
Dar. 18/10-15/11/56.**G.**
Dar. 4/11/58. *Not repaired.*

BOILERS:
5D3177.
Renumbered 128 28/6/35.
  1990 *(ex249)* 26/7/37.
  2654 *(ex220)* 6/3/40.
  2768 *(ex353)* 9/9/43.
  7965 *(ex297)* 30/3/46.
  4006 *(new)* 26/10/49.
  27382 *(ex2725)* 12/10/51.
  27407 *(ex2765)* 15/11/56.

SHEDS:
York.
Gateshead 29/9/46.
Bridlington 12/3/50.
Hull Botanic Gardens 9/1/55.
Bridlington 29/9/55.
Hull Botanic Gardens 22/9/57.

RENUMBERED:
2750 1/12/46.
62750 26/10/49.

CONDEMNED:
4/11/58.

205 THE ALBRIGHTON

Darlington.

To traffic 10/7/34.

REPAIRS:
Dar. 18/11/35-13/1/36.**G.**
Heat.conn.at front.
Dar. 24/5-1/7/37.**G.**
Dar. 19/10-7/12/38.**G.** *After collision.*
Dar. 23/10-20/11/40.**N/C.**
Dar. 15/5-24/6/41.**G.**
Dar. 25-27/6/41.**N/C.**
Dar. 27/4-21/5/43.**L.**
Cow. 23/2-15/4/44.**G.**
Cow. 15/9-13/10/45.**G.**
Ghd. 10-20/12/46.**L.**
Dar. 28/4-11/6/48.**G.**
Dar. 15-23/6/48. *Tender only.*
Dar. 26/6-6/7/48.**N/C.**
Dar. 2/12/49-12/1/50.**G.**
Dar. 2-30/11/51.**G.**
Dar. 4/3-19/9/53.**G.**
Dar. 7/10-5/11/55.**G.**
Dar. 9-10/11/55.**N/C.**
Dar. 11/10-9/11/57.**G.**
Dar. 11-16/11/57.**N/C.**
Dar. 17-25/3/58.**C/L.**
Dar. 12-23/9/58.**C/L.**
Dar. 13/3/59. *Not repaired.*

BOILERS:
2594.
2031 *(ex236)* 13/1/36.
  127 *(ex297)* 1/7/37.

2599 *(ex368)* 7/12/38.
7950 *(ex201)* 24/6/41.
2631 *(ex292)* 15/4/44.
3810 *(new)* 11/6/48.
3789 *(ex2707)* 12/1/50.
27388 *(ex2744)* 30/11/51.
27362 *(ex2775)* 19/9/53.
27398 *(ex2720)* 5/11/55.
27421 *(ex2714)* 9/11/57.

SHEDS:
Hull Botanic Gardens.
York 31/5/39.
Scarborough 13/6/48.

RENUMBERED:
2751 2/6/46.
62751 11/6/48.

CONDEMNED:
13/3/59.

214 THE ATHERSTONE

Darlington.

To traffic 14/7/34.

REPAIRS:
Dar. 18/11/35-21/1/36.**G.**
Heat.conn.at front.
Dar. 9/3-7/4/36. *Tender only.*
Dar. 3/11-23/12/37.**G.** *'Syntholux' paint.*
Dar. 27/4-17/6/39.**G.**
Dar. 4/2-13/3/41.**G.**
Dar. 23/9-23/10/42.**G.**
Don. 31/10-6/11/42.**L.**
Cow. 1/1-10/2/45.**G.**
Dar. 19/10/46-11/1/47.**G.**

Dar. 18-24/1/47.**N/C.**
Dar. 8-13/2/47.**N/C.**
Dar. 14/3-12/4/48.**L.**
Dar. 22/3-28/4/49.**G.**
Dar. 2-18/5/49.**N/C.**
Dar. 20-30/5/49.**N/C.**
Dar. 15/5-9/6/51.**G.**
Dar. 11-12/6/51.**N/C.**
Dar. 26-27/6/51.**N/C.**
Dar. 14/7-27/8/53.**G.**
Dar. 22/7-24/9/55.**G.**
Dar. 28/9-4/10/55.**N/C.**
Dar. 29/7/58. *Not repaired.*

BOILERS:
2592.
2594 *(ex205)* 21/1/36.
2592 *(ex217)* 23/12/37.
2014 *(ex376)* 17/6/39.
7965 *(ex376)* 13/3/41.
2613 *(ex232)* 23/10/42.
1996 *(ex376)* 10/2/45.
1998 *(ex322)* 11/1/47.
2615 *(ex2733)* 28/4/49.
27374 *(ex2715)* 9/6/51.
27372 *(ex2764)* 27/8/53.
27365 *(ex2742)* 24/9/55.

SHEDS:
Hull Botanic Gardens.
Neville Hill 19/4/45.
Starbeck 5/10/47.

RENUMBERED:
2752 31/3/46.
62752 12/4/48.

CONDEMNED:
29/7/58.

217 THE BELVOIR

Darlington.

To traffic 17/7/34.

REPAIRS:
Dar. 9-17/8/34.**N/C.**
Dar. 21-30/8/34.**N/C.**
Dar. 5/12/35-8/2/36.**G.**
Dar. 22/6-24/8/37.**G.**
Dar. 6/3-22/4/39.**G.**
Dar. 3/1-18/2/41.**G.**
Dar. 3/11-3/12/42.**G.**
Cow. 27/4-3/6/44.**G.**
Cow. 31/3-19/5/45.**L.**
Cow. 4-11/8/45.**L.**
Dar. 29/11/46-25/1/47.**G.**
Dar. 5-15/2/47.**N/C.**
Ghd. 24/3-16/4/48.**L.**
Dar. 2/5-3/6/49.**G.**
Dar. 1-2/11/49. *Weigh.*
Dar. 25/10-25/11/50.**L/I.**
Dar. 27-29/11/50.**N/C.**

Dar. 20/5-19/7/52.**G.**
Dar. 12/7/54-5/3/55.**G.**
Dar. 7-9/3/55.**N/C.**
Dar. 18-23/3/55.**N/C.**
Dar. 25/3-26/4/57.**G.**
Dar. 15/8-17/9/57.**C/L.**

BOILERS:
2596.
2592 *(ex214)* 8/2/36.
2031 *(ex205)* 24/8/37.
2597 *(ex222)* 22/4/39.
2953 *(ex226)* 18/2/41.
2614 *(ex269)* 3/12/42.
2019 *(ex329)* 3/6/44.
1931 *(ex2993)* 25/1/47.
3972 *(new)* 3/6/49.
3972 *Ren.* 27359 25/11/50.
27395 *(ex2717)* 5/3/55.
27375 *(ex2733)* 26/4/57.

SHEDS:
Neville Hill.
Starbeck 5/10/47.
York 13/9/59.

RENUMBERED:
2753 28/4/46.
62753 16/4/48.

CONDEMNED:
22/9/59.

222 THE BERKELEY

Darlington.

To traffic 20/7/34.

REPAIRS:
Dar. 19/6-3/9/36.**G.**
Dar. 5-18/9/36.**N/C.** *Heat.conn.at front.*
Dar. 12/5-29/6/38.**G.**
Dar. 18/6-16/7/40.**G.**
Dar. 3-31/10/42.**G.**
Cow. 5/2-10/3/45.**G.**
Cow. 25/8-29/9/45.**L.**
Cow. 27/7-12/10/46.**G.**
Dar. 3-25/3/47.**L.**
Ghd. 9-24/10/47.**L.**
Dar. 10/11/48-5/1/49.**G.**
Dar. 31/1/49. *Weigh.*
Dar. 28/7-26/8/50.**G.**
Dar. 7/5-6/6/52.**G.**
Dar. 8-17/4/53.**C/L.**
Dar. 23/12/53-26/6/54.**G.**
Dar. 1/4-2/5/57.**G.**
Dar. 3/11/58. *Not repaired.*

BOILERS:
2597.
2777 *(ex258)* 29/6/38.
2125 *(ex368)* 16/7/40.
2607 *(ex336)* 31/10/42.

Every D49 was fitted for applying sand by gravity to the front of the leading coupled wheels, but it was found that when they had to reverse up Cowlairs incline after working into Glasgow (Queen Street) sanding was needed behind the rear coupled wheels. From March 1933 Cowlairs added rear sanding to fifteen Part 1 shedded at Eastfield, Haymarket and St Margarets, those concerned being 264, 265, 270, 277, 281, 306, 311, 2753, 2754, 2755, 2756, 2757, 2758, 2759 and 2760. *Photomatic*

No other D49 acquired back sanding for another ten years, but between September 1943 and October 1946, the whole class had at least one heavy repair at Cowlairs. In that period they added it to three Part 1 and to fourteen Part 2 whilst they were there for repairs. 62763, then as 359 THE FITZWILLIAM, had a general repair at Cowlairs in November 1944, but missed being fitted for back sanding, and was never so equipped as evidenced in this view of it at Hull Dairycoates on 20th August 1960. Fitting of sanding to aid running in reverse ceased in 1946, and there were no subsequent additions. *P.H.Groom*

2332 *(ex234)* 12/10/46.
2631 *(ex2765)* 26/8/50.
27408 *(ex2759)* 6/6/52.
27394 *(ex2762)* 2/5/57.

SHEDS:
Scarborough.
Hull Botanic Gardens 29/11/34.
Scarborough 1/7/35.
York 28/11/40.
Hull Botanic Gardens 8/10/45.

RENUMBERED:
2754 12/10/46.
62754 5/1/49.

CONDEMNED:
3/11/58.

226 THE BILSDALE

Darlington.

To traffic 23/7/34.

REPAIRS:
Dar. 28/8-19/10/36.**G.**
Dar. 15-21/6/37.**N/C.** *Heat.conn.at front.*
Dar. 21/9-28/10/38.**G.**
Dar. 30/10-4/12/40.**G.**
Dar. 22/6-7/8/43.**G.**
Dar. 9-11/8/43.**N/C.**
Cow. 6-27/1/45.**G.**
Dar. 14/10-28/11/47.**G.**
Dar. 16-31/12/47.**N/C.**
Ghd. 28/7-29/8/49.**C/L.**
Dar. 29/8-29/9/50.**G.**

Dar. 29/9-25/10/52.**G.**
Dar. 27/10-5/11/52.**N/C.**
Dar. 19/6-26/7/54.**C/H.**
Dar. 11/7-9/9/55.**G.**
Dar. 5/2-14/3/57.**C/L.** *After colln.*
Dar. 12/11/58. *Not repaired.*

BOILERS:
2598.
2044 *(ex336)* 19/10/36.
2953 *(new)* 28/10/38.
2777 *(ex222)* 4/12/40.
127 *(ex255)* 7/8/43.
2024 *(ex273)* 27/1/45.
1985 *(ex336)* 28/11/47.
27353 *(ex2754)* 29/9/50.
27430 *(new)* 25/10/52.

SHEDS:
Scarborough.
York 27/11/40.
Scarborough 13/6/48.
Starbeck 27/11/49.
Neville Hill 3/6/56.
Selby 23/9/56.

RENUMBERED:
2755 23/6/46.
62755 29/8/49.

CONDEMNED:
12/11/58.

230 THE BROCKLESBY

Darlington.

To traffic 10/8/34.

REPAIRS:
Dar. 8/7-27/8/36.**G.**
Dar. 9/3-6/5/38.**G.** *Heat.conn.at front.*
Dar. 13/3-17/4/40.**G.**
Dar. 27/7-13/9/41.**G.**
Dar. 22/4-22/5/43.**G.**
Dar. 24-28/5/43.**N/C.**
Cow. 30/10-9/12/44.**G.**
Dar. 5/10/46-8/2/47.**G.**
Ghd. 12-23/1/48.**L.**
Dar. 31/5-30/6/49.**G.**
Dar. 18/1-16/2/52.**G.**
Dar. 5/6/53. *Weigh.*
Dar. 15/9-14/10/53.**G.**
Dar. 20-22/10/53.**N/C.**
Dar. 30/11-11/12/54.**C/L.**
Dar. 22/11-17/12/55.**G.**
Dar. 30/4/58. *Not repaired.*

BOILERS:
2599.
2768 *(new)* 27/8/36.
2594 *(ex214)* 6/5/38.
1990 *(ex298)* 17/4/40.
1985 *(ex283)* 13/9/41.
8010 *(ex1487)* 22/5/43.
2051 *(ex2757)* 8/2/47.
2947 *(ex2720)* 30/6/49.
27398 *(ex2769)* 16/2/52.
27383 *(ex2710)* 14/10/53.
27825 *(new)* 17/12/55.

SHEDS:
Bridlington.
Hull Botanic Gardens 17/4/35.
Neville Hill 10/6/39.
Scarborough 1/7/51.

REPAIRS:
Dar. 8/7-27/8/36.**G.**
Dar. 9/3-6/5/38.**G.** *Heat.conn.at front.*

RENUMBERED:
2756 16/6/46.
62756 30/6/49.

CONDEMNED:
30/4/58.

238 THE BURTON

Darlington.

To traffic 17/8/34.

REPAIRS:
Dar. 19/3-9/5/36.**G.**
Dar. 1/11-17/12/37.**G.**
Dar. 21/9-28/10/39.**G.**
Dar. 29/5-12/7/41.**G.**
Dar. 18/3-14/4/43.**G.**
Cow. 16/9-11/11/44.**G.**
Cow. 5/1-9/2/46.**G.** *Rear sanding fitted.*
Cow. 2-30/3/46.**L.**
Ghd. 25/1-8/2/47.**L.**
Dar. 7/7-27/8/48.**G.**
Dar. 31/8-13/9/48.**N/C.**
Dar. 5-26/11/48.**L.**
Dar. 26/1-23/2/49.**L.**
Dar. 9/8-8/9/50.**G.**
Dar. 14-21/9/50.**N/C.**
Dar. 8/7-16/8/52.**G.**
Dar. 18-19/8/52.**N/C.**
Dar. 26/1-20/2/54.**G.**
Dar. 31/12/54-25/1/55.**N/C.**
Dar. 1/12/55-4/1/56.**G.**
Dar. 10/12/57. *Not repaired.*

INVERNESS-SHIRE had a general repair at Cowlairs in April 1944, and another in October 1945, so why it did not get back sanding is puzzling, when it was shedded at Perth from May 1940 and did work into Glasgow (Queen Street) station. Here at Stirling in October 1958, it is clearly on its last wheels, and awaiting the call to be scrapped. *WBY collection*

BOILERS:
2600.
1987 *(ex264)* 9/5/36.
2608 *(ex376)* 17/12/37.
124 *(ex279)* 28/10/39.
2041 *(ex235)* 12/7/41.
2125 *(ex222)* 14/4/43.
2952 *(ex235)* 9/2/46.
2591 *(ex2762)* 27/8/48.
27350 *(ex2749)* 8/9/50.
27407 *(ex2706)* 16/8/52.
27393 *(ex2737)* 20/2/54.
27377 *(ex2748)* 4/1/56.

SHEDS:
Bridlington.
Hull Botanic Gardens 17/4/35.

RENUMBERED:
2757 12/5/46.
62757 27/8/48.

CONDEMNED:
10/12/57.

258 THE CATTISTOCK

Darlington.

To traffic 22/8/34.

REPAIRS:
Dar. 7/5-3/7/36.**G.**

Dar. 21/4-3/6/38.**G.**
Dar. 30/9-7/11/40.**G.**
Dar. 30/3-4/5/43.**G.**
Cow. 19/2-17/3/45.**G.**
Dar. 14/9-8/10/45.**L.**
Dar. 7/3-26/4/47.**G.**
Dar. 24/10-7/11/47.**L.**
Dar. 3-25/3/48.**L.**
Ghd. 12/7-6/8/48.**L.**
Dar. 22/8-21/9/49.**G.**
Ghd. 28/9-30/9/49.**N/C.**
Dar. 8/6-6/7/51.**G.**
Dar. 10/4-16/5/53.**H/I.**
Dar. 18-19/5/53.**N/C.**
Dar. 7/6-10/12/55.**G.**
Dar. 12-13/12/55.**N/C.**
Dar. 11/12/57. *Not repaired.*

BOILERS:
2601.
2777 *(new)* 3/7/36.
2768 *(ex230)* 3/6/38.
2594 *(ex230)* 7/11/40.
2950 *(ex1536)* 4/5/43.
127 *(ex226)* 17/3/45.
3776 *(new)* 26/4/47.
2599 *(ex2722)* 21/9/49.
27356 *(new)* 6/7/51.
27366 *(ex2707)* 10/12/55.

SHEDS:
Scarborough.
York 31/5/39.
Neville Hill 2/6/43.

Starbeck 15/8/48.

RENUMBERED:
2758 1/12/46.
62758 25/3/48.

CONDEMNED:
11/12/57.

274 THE CRAVEN

Darlington.

To traffic 28/8/34.

REPAIRS:
Dar. 7/1-7/3/36.**G.**
Dar. 24/8-8/10/37.**G.** *Heat.conn.at front.*
Dar. 5/4-12/5/39.**G.**
Dar. 6/2-20/3/41.**G.**
Dar. 20/2-10/4/43.**G.**
Cow. 10-31/3/45.**G.**
Dar. 24/8-21/9/46.**L.**
Dar. 20/9-23/10/47.**G.**
Dar. 5-17/11/47.**N/C.**
Ghd. 10-25/1/49.**L.**
Dar. 3/1-15/4/50.**G.**
Dar. 19/2-21/3/52.**G.**
Dar. 17/8-19/9/53.**N/C.**
Dar. 6/4-54. *Weigh.*
Dar. 1/10-13/11/54.**G.**
Dar. 26/5-7/6/56.**C/H.**

Dar. 12/11-7/12/56.**G.**
Dar. 8-28/1/57.**C/L.**
Dar. 13/1/61. *Not repaired.*

BOILERS:
2602.
7956 *Renumbered 7966 (ex282)* 7/3/36.
2596 *(ex282)* 8/10/37.
2046 *(ex306)* 12/5/39.
2626 *(ex255)* 20/3/41.
2000 *(ex376)* 10/4/43.
2002 *(ex201)* 31/3/45.
2627 *(ex253)* 23/10/47.
3810 *(ex2751)* 15/4/50.
27403 *(ex2726)* 21/3/52.
27410 *(ex2744)* 7/12/56.

SHEDS:
Scarborough.
York 26/11/40.
Scarborough 2/6/43.
York 12/3/45.
Starbeck 5/12/54.
Hull Dairycoates 13/9/59.

RENUMBERED:
2759 24/11/46.
62759 25/1/49.

CONDEMNED:
13/1/61.

When new, all had this type of smokebox door which was only slightly dished, and its outer rim a flat flange. The straps were of Darlington design with split hinges, and 270 ARGYLLSHIRE shows the pattern used until 1943. *E.V.Fry*

When smokebox door, or front, needed replacing after May 1943, a modified design was used. That was more dished, had no flat flange, but was sealed by a pressed joint ring. There was no alteration however to the type of hinge strap. Ex works in August 1947, ARGYLLSHIRE, now renumbered 2708, had been changed to the later type of door. *E.V.Fry*

The standard fastening for both types of smokebox door was a pair of handles, and all were so fitted when new. But a reversion to pre-Grouping North Eastern method did creep in on D49 class, a wheel replacing one of the handles, as seen on 236 LANCASHIRE in 1932. It was seen later on a couple of Part 2 engines, 336 having wheel and handle in the mid-1930's, and in 1938, 359 was so fitted, but the wheel then disappeared from D49 class. *Photomatic*

When the first 28 were built it was necessary to fit them for train braking by air as well as by vacuum. The cylindrical air receiver was fixed under the rear end of the tender as here on 245 LINCOLNSHIRE. Note also the two standpipes for train connections, the larger one for vacuum and the smaller for Westinghouse air brake. Doncaster having built the tenders is the reason why *two* lamp irons were fitted at the near side rear corner. They were for use by some Great Northern London District train indication codes, already defunct before Grouping, but it was into the 1930's before Doncaster ceased fitting the one that was redundant. Tenders carrying both irons were certainly to be seen working on D49s in Scottish Area. *WBY collection*

The Unification of Brakes Programme proceeded sufficiently fast for the Westinghouse air brake to be dispensed with on D49 class from March 1930 (no.307) to May 1933 (no.250). No.329 here has neither pump nor front end connecting hose - they were removed in March 1933. *WBY collection*

The eight Part 1 built in 1929, and the ten Part 2 in 1932 (which included no.235 THE BEDALE) had steam brake on engine with vacuum ejector for train brakes. So at the front end there was only the vacuum standpipe until train heating connection was added from March 1935. *Photomatic*

Only the last five Part 2 had front heater connection from new but, when convenient, it was added to the earlier engines, although it was not until February 1939 when fitting of no.353 THE DERWENT completed that job. Here, Leeds based, 217 THE BELVOIR shows its new connection after its 'general' in 1937. *WBY collection*

One of the bonuses for enthusiasts was spotting an 'odd man out', and that certainly applied to 62729 as seen at St Margarets on 11th August 1960. Only on Parts 2 and 3 were outside steam pipes fitted, but this Part 1 engine had acquired a smokebox saddle from one of them as shown by the gap in its top edge. It was so fitted ex works 30th November 1957, and by then three of Part 2 had reached Darlington for dismembering. *P.H.Groom*

All D49 class built prior to May 1932, and also nos.201 and 211 had drainpipes from the cylinders terminating by the rim of the leading wheel of the bogie, and on the Part 1 engines the linkage for operating them was ahead of the cylinders. *LPC*

The six Part 3 engines had the same short length cylinder drain pipes, but the operating linkage for them was at the rear end of the cylinders. 327 is at York in July 1928. *W.Potter*

When those Part 3 engines were rebuilt to Part 1 in 1938 they conformed to the latter by having their cylinder drain pipe linkage moved to ahead of the cylinders. *WBY collection*

Beginning with no.220 THE ZETLAND in May 1932, the cylinder drain pipes were extended to just ahead of the buffer beam, and so were able to be clipped to the front footsteps for support. The earlier engines then changed gradually to the longer pipes. All Part 2 engines, including 336 and 352, had the operating linkage at the rear of the cylinders. *WBY collection*

279 THE COTSWOLD

Darlington.

To traffic 3/9/34.

REPAIRS:
Dar. 18/2-3/4/36.**G.**
Dar. 25/10-9/12/37.**G.**
Dar. 22-31/12/37.**N/C.**
Dar. 16/3-12/4/38.**N/C.**
Dar. 1/6-7/7/39.**G.**
Dar. 27/7-9/8/39.**N/C.**
Dar. 11-18/9/39.**N/C.**
Dar. 25/2-10/4/41.**G.**
Cow. 3-28/12/43.**G.**
Cow. 8/6-13/7/46.**G.**
Ghd. 2-26/9/47.**L.**
Dar. 7/5-15/6/49.**G.**
Dar. 13/12/51-12/1/52.**H/I.**
Dar. 8/7-7/8/54.**G.**
Dar. 6/7-23/8/57.**G.**

BOILERS:
2603.
2038 (ex253) 3/4/36.
124 (ex283) 9/12/37.
2031 (ex217) 7/7/39.
2174 (ex353) 10/4/41.
125 (ex362) 28/12/43.
2038 (ex2754) 13/7/46.
3974 (new) 15/6/49.
3974 Ren. 27401 12/1/52.
27389 (ex2745) 7/8/54.
27440 (ex2747) 23/8/57.

SHEDS:
Scarborough.
York 27/11/40.
Hull Botanic Gardens 8/6/58.
Hull Dairycoates 14/6/59.

RENUMBERED:
2760 24/11/46.
62760 15/6/49.

CONDEMNED:
21/10/59.

353 THE DERWENT

Darlington.

To traffic 12/9/34.

REPAIRS:
Dar. 30/10-16/12/36.**G.**
Dar. 5/1-9/2/39.**G.**
Dar. 3/12/40-8/1/41.**G.**
Dar. 19/4-20/5/43.**G.**
Cow. 6-27/10/45.**G.**
Dar. 25/6-27/8/48.**G.**
Dar. 8/1-17/2/51.**G.**

Dar. 12/12/52-10/1/53.**G.**
Dar. 12-13/1/53.**N/C.**
Dar. 24-27/2/53.**N/C.**
Dar. 25/2-21/5/55.**G.**

BOILERS:
2604.
7965 (ex273) 16/12/36.
2174 (ex365) 9/2/39.
2768 (ex258) 8/1/41.
2594 (ex258) 20/5/43.
2148 (ex2760) 27/10/45.
2594 (ex2770) 27/8/48.
2594 Ren. 27366 17/2/51.
27358 (ex2767) 10/1/53.

SHEDS:
Scarborough.
York 27/11/40.
Starbeck 1/10/50.
Neville Hill 8/7/56.
Selby 23/9/56.

RENUMBERED:
2761 3/11/46.
62761 27/8/48.

CONDEMNED:
6/12/57.

357 THE FERNIE

Darlington.

To traffic 22/9/34.

REPAIRS:
Dar. 12/8-3/10/36.**G.**
Dar. 5-14/10/36.**N/C.**
Dar. 7/3-4/5/38.**G.** Heat.conn.at front.
Dar. 14/2-18/3/40.**G.**
Dar. 14/5-25/6/41.**G.**
Dar. 5/12/42-8/1/43.**G.**
Cow. 22/7-26/8/44.**G.**
Cow. 9/3-4/5/46.**G.** Rear sanding fitted.
Dar. 7/9-16/10/46.**L.** After collision.
Ghd. 13-24/4/47.**L.**
Dar. 26/2-7/4/48.**G.**
Dar. 12/4-7/5/48.**N/C.**
Dar. 7/8-5/11/48.**L.** After collision.
Dar. 19/6-14/7/50.**G.**
Dar. 4/4-3/5/52.**H/I.**
Dar. 17/6-16/7/54.**G.**
Dar. 16/1-14/2/57.**G.**
Dar. 13/10/60.Not repaired.

BOILERS:
2605.
2626 (ex370) 3/10/36.
7964 (ex364) 4/5/38.

2600 (ex374) 18/3/40.
2014 (ex214) 25/6/41.
2953 (ex217) 8/1/43.
7952 (ex361) 26/8/44.
2591 (ex1587) 4/5/46.
128 (ex329) 7/4/48.
3800 (ex2717) 14/7/50.
3800 Renumbered 27412 3/5/52.
27394 (ex2773) 16/7/54.
27826 (new) 14/2/57.

SHEDS:
Neville Hill.
Starbeck 12/12/47.
Scarborough 8/6/58.

RENUMBERED:
2762 24/11/46.
62762 7/4/48.

CONDEMNED:
13/10/60.

359 THE FITZWILLIAM

Darlington.

To traffic 28/9/34.

REPAIRS:
Dar. 2/6-11/7/36.**G.**
Dar. 14/2-8/4/38.**G.**
Dar. 8/11-20/12/39.**G.**
Dar. 3-25/9/40.**N/C.**
Dar. 4-25/11/40.**L.** After collision.
Dar. 15/4-13/5/42.**G.**
Cow. 2-25/11/44.**G.**
Dar. 6/8-6/9/47.**G.**
Dar. 20/9-19/10/49.**G.**
Dar. 25/10-2/11/49.**N/C.**
Dar. 17/10-17/11/51.**G.**
Dar. 19-20/11/51.**N/C.**
Dar. 1-31/10/53.**G.**
Dar. 2-9/6/54.**C/L.**
Dar. 17/11-17/12/55.**G.**
Dar. 8/11-31/12/57.**G.**
Dar. 31/10-13/11/58.**N/C.**
Dar. 16/1/61.Not repaired.

BOILERS:
2606.
2634 (ex365) 20/12/39.
2034 (ex273) 13/5/42.
2596 (ex370) 25/11/44.
3809 (new) 6/9/47.
3776 (ex2758) 19/10/49.
27390 (ex2750) 17/11/51.
27364 (ex2729) 31/10/53.
27376 (ex2723) 17/12/55.
27398 (ex2751) 31/12/57.

SHEDS:
York.
Starbeck 26/2/48.
Hull Dairycoates 13/9/59.

RENUMBERED:
2763 17/11/46.
62763 19/10/49.

CONDEMNED:
16/1/61.

361 THE GARTH

Darlington.

To traffic 2/10/34.

REPAIRS:
Dar. 18/3-18/4/35.**L.**
Dar. 26/6-24/8/36.**G.**
Dar. 21/12/36-5/2/37.**N/C.**
Dar. 7/6-29/7/38.**G.**
Dar. 23/1-3/3/39.**H.**
Dar. 12/12/39-2/2/40.**N/C.**
Dar. 5/6-9/7/40.**G.**
Dar. 25/4-23/5/42.**G.**
Dar. 30/7-28/8/43.**L.**
Dar. 20/12/43-15/1/44.**L.**
Cow. 1/7-5/8/44.**G.**
Cow. 12-26/5/45.**L.**
Dar. 21-31/7/45.**L.**
Cow. 17/11/45-23/2/46.**G.** Rear sanding fitted.
Cow. 23-30/3/46.**L.**
Dar. 8/3-22/4/48.**L.**
Dar. 26/11/48-19/2/49.**G.** Infinitely variable valve gear fitted.
Dar. 23-30/3/49.**N/C.**
Dar. 8-20/4/49.**N/C.**
Dar. 28-30/4/49.**N/C.** Prepared for test at Rugby.
Dar. 7-9/9/49.**N/C.** To remove test gear.
Dar. 28/1-20/2/50.**C/L.**
Dar. 14-23/9/50.**C/L.**
Dar. 19/10-4/11/50.**C/L.**
Dar. 14/2-1/3/51.**C/L.**
Dar. 27/3-26/4/51.**G.**
Dar. 27/3-12/5/53.**G.**
Dar. 26/11/53-13/4/54.**N/C.**
Dar. 15/9-19/10/55.**G.**
Dar. 15/9-19/10/55.**G.**
Dar. 8-22/11/55.**N/C.**
Dar. 13/11/58.Not repaired.

BOILERS:
2607.
1996 (ex277) 29/7/38.
2606 (ex359) 9/7/40.
7952 (ex292) 23/5/42.
2044 (ex377) 5/8/44.
2913 (ex2700) 19/2/49.

WORKS CODES:- Cow - Cowlairs. Dar - Darlington. Don - Doncaster. Ghd - Gateshead. Gor - Gorton. Inv - Inverurie. Str - Stratford.
REPAIR CODES:- **C/H** - Casual Heavy. **C/L** - Casual Light. **G** - General. **H** - Heavy. **H/I** - Heavy Intermediate. **L** - Light. **L/I** - Light Intermediate. **N/C** - Non-Classified.

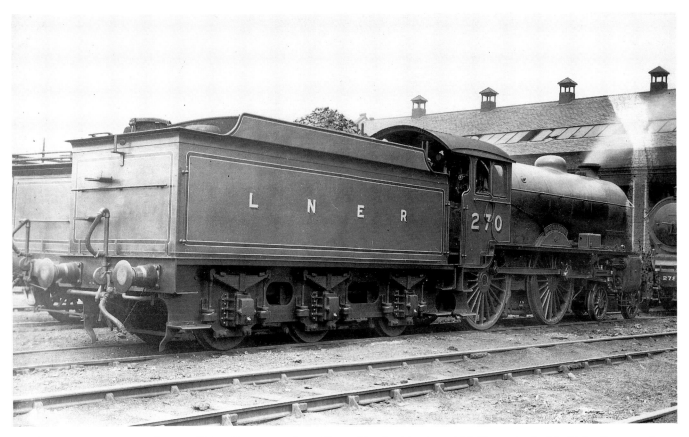

The first 28 were coupled with the 4200 gallons stepped top Group Standard tender, which Doncaster had built for them, as shown here with no.270 in early 1931. They carried a 5" x 3" plate at the rear under the coping which showed a number in the 5295 to 5322 range of Doncaster tender numbers. Note the useless extra lamp iron at the near side. *WBY collection*

27372 (*ex2771*) 26/4/51.
27423 (*ex2768*) 12/5/53.
27372 (*ex2752*) 19/10/55.

SHEDS:
Gateshead.
Scarborough 11/9/49.
Neville Hill 1/7/51.

RENUMBERED:
2764 27/10/46.
62764 22/4/48.

CONDEMNED:
13/11/58.

362 THE GOATHLAND

Darlington.

To traffic 11/10/34.

REPAIRS:
Dar. 6/1-20/3/36.**G.**
Dar. 24/6-26/8/37.**G.** *Heat.conn.at front.*
Dar. 8/3-5/5/39.**G.**
Dar. 17/1-28/2/41.**G.**
Cow. 16/11-4/12/43.**G.**
Dar. 10/8-12/10/46.**G.**
Dar. 7-28/11/46.**N/C.**

Dar. 2/6-2/7/48.**G.**
Dar. 5-15/7/48.**N/C.**
Dar. 26/5-24/6/50.**G.**
Dar. 26-27/6/50.**N/C.**
Dar. 5-13/7/50.**N/C.**
Dar. 18/6-9/8/52.**G.**
Dar. 11-12/8/52.**N/C.**
Dar. 22/6-16/7/54.**G.**
Dar. 21/7-4/8/54.**N/C.**
Dar. 9-11/8/54.**N/C.**
Dar. 27/4-31/5/56.**G.**
Dar. 21/4-16/5/58.**G.**
Dar. 16/9-1/10/58.**N/C.**
Dar. 16/1/61.*Not repaired.*

BOILERS:
2608.
2602 (*ex274*) 20/3/36.
128 (*ex298*) 26/8/37.
2002 (*ex288*) 5/5/39.
125 (*ex297*) 28/2/41.
2765 (*ex235*) 4/12/43.
2631 (*ex205*) 2/7/48.
2606 (*ex2773*) 24/6/50.
27413 (*ex2723*) 9/8/52.
27407 (*ex2757*) 16/7/54.
27392 (*ex2710*) 31/5/56.
27436 (*ex2711*) 16/5/58.

SHEDS:
Gateshead.
Alston 27/5/40.

Tweedmouth 2/11/40.
Neville Hill 23/7/45.
Starbeck 24/2/48.
Selby 14/6/59.
Hull Dairycoates 13/9/59.

RENUMBERED:
2765 12/10/46.
62765 2/7/48.

CONDEMNED:
16/1/61.

363 THE GRAFTON

Darlington.

To traffic 15/11/34.

REPAIRS:
Dar. 21/4-9/6/36.**G.**
Dar. 13/1-19/2/38.**G.** *Heat.conn.at front.*
Dar. 7/9-19/10/39.**G.**
Dar. 6-29/11/39.**N/C.**
Dar. 10/11-20/12/41.**G.**
Cow. 8-29/10/43.**G.**
Cow. 17-19/8/44.**L.**
Dar. 13/8-5/10/46.**G.**
Dar. 25/10-6/11/46.**N/C.**
Ghd. 13/5-14/6/47.**L.**

Dar. 7/7-13/8/48.**L.**
Ghd. 31/8-7/10/49.**C/L.**
Dar. 30/3-12/5/50.**G.**
Dar. 14/11/51-18/1/52.**G.**
Dar. 29/9-24/10/53.**G.**
Dar. 26-27/10/53.**N/C.**
Dar. 9-10/11/53.**N/C.**
Dar. 16/10-5/11/54.**N/C.**
Dar. 9/12/54-15/1/55.**C/L.**
Dar. 27/1-28/2/56.**G.**
Dar. 30/9/58.*Not repaired.*

BOILERS:
2611.
2615 (*ex366*) 9/6/36.
128 (*ex362*) 19/10/39.
2023 (*ex352*) 20/12/41.
3799 (*ex2738*) 12/5/50.
3799 Ren. 27397 18/1/52.
27361 (*ex2705*) 24/10/53.
27383 (*ex2756*) 28/2/56.

SHEDS:
Gateshead.
Bridlington 12/3/50.
Hull Botanic Gardens 9/1/55.
Bridlington 29/5/55.
Hull Botanic Gardens 10/6/56.

RENUMBERED:
2766 10/11/46.
62766 13/8/48.

In 1938 to 1942 all except one of these Doncaster built tenders was taken from D49 class to save building tenders for V2 and 02 class engines then under construction. The only D49 not so denuded was Part 2 no.352 THE MEYNELL which, as 2726 and 62726, retained that variety through to its December 1957 withdrawal. Until September 1934 it had tender 5319, and during a repair it exchanged with engine 329, acquiring 5304 which is the one here. 62726 is at Croft Spa. *Photomatic*

363 continued
CONDEMNED:
30/9/58.

364 THE GROVE

Darlington.

To traffic 19/11/34.

REPAIRS:
Dar. 14/4-6/6/36.**G.**
Dar. 9/12/37-15/2/38.**G.**
Heat.conn.at front.
Dar. 23/8-27/9/39.**G.**
Dar. 23/10-14/11/40.**N/C.**
Dar. 26/6-23/8/41.**G.**
Dar. 28/5-5/9/41.**N/C.**
Dar. 24/8-4/9/42.**N/C.**
Cow. 11/4-6/5/44.**G.**
Dar. 2/10-15/11/46.**G.**
Dar. 26/11-5/12/46.**N/C.**
Dar. 14-30/1/47.**N/C.**
Dar. 2/7-15/8/47.**L.**
Ghd. 1-19/3/48.**L.**
Dar. 7/3-14/4/49.**G.**
Dar. 19-21/4/49.**N/C.**
Dar. 10/2-9/3/51.**G.**
Dar. 13/11-11/12/52.**G.**
Dar. 15/10-18/11/53.**C/L.**

Dar. 22/9-23/10/54.**G.**
Dar. 26-28/10/54.**N/C.**
Dar. 9-10/11/54.**N/C.**
Dar. 15/3-13/4/57.**G.**
Dar. 20/10/58.*Not repaired.*

BOILERS:
2613.
7964 *(ex322)* 6/6/36.
1987 *(ex238)* 15/2/38.
2596 *(ex274)* 27/9/39.
2599 *(ex205)* 23/8/41.
7951 *(ex Darl.)* 6/5/44.
2953 *(ex273)* 15/11/46.
132 *(ex282)* 14/4/49.
27358 *(new)* 9/3/51.
27368 *(ex2720)* 11/12/52.
27413 *(ex2765)* 23/10/54.
27412 *(ex2700)* 13/4/57.

SHEDS:
Gateshead.
Hull Botanic Gardens 12/5/46.

RENUMBERED:
2767 15/11/46.
62767 14/4/49.

CONDEMNED:
20/10/58.

365 THE MORPETH

Darlington.

To traffic 1/12/34.

REPAIRS:
Dar. 13/9-29/11/35. *Tender only.After collision.*
Dar. 23/9-11/11/36.**G.**
Dar. 1-22/3/37.**L.**
Dar. 28/4-19/5/37.**N/C.**
Dar. 22/6-19/8/38.**G.**
Dar. 21/9-24/1/40.**G.**
Dar. 26/1-12/2/40.**N/C.**
Dar. 20/2-9/3/40.**N/C.**
Dar. 19/3-1/4/40.**N/C.**
Dar. 18/4-29/5/40.**N/C.**
Dar. 26/8-13/9/40.**N/C.**
Dar. 24/9-8/10/40.**N/C.**
Dar. 27/2/41-24/8/42.**G.** *Rebuilt to part 4.*
Dar. 2-16/9/42.**L.**
Dar. 23/9-2/10/42.**N/C.**
Dar. 12-16/10/42.**N/C.**
Dar. 1-16/2/43.**N/C.**
Dar. 12/11-7/12/43. *Spec.exam.*
Dar. 11/12/43-8/1/44.**N/C.**
Dar. 18/5-20/6/44.**N/C.**
Dar. 24/7-31/8/44.**G.**
Dar. 10/11-7/12/45.**L.**

Dar. 17-26/1/46.**L.**
Dar. 14/4-17/5/47.**G.**
Dar. 3/7/47-19/8/48.**L.** *Fractured frame.*
Dar. 18/5-13/7/50.**G.**
Dar. 23/10/52. *Not repaired.After collision.*

BOILERS:
2614.
2174 *(ex2757)* 11/11/36.
2634 *(ex377)* 19/8/38.
1987 *(ex364)* 24/1/40.
3782 *(new)* 17/5/47.
2627 *(ex2759)* 13/7/50.

SHEDS:
Gateshead.
Neville Hill 13/12/34.
Haymarket 27/11/42.
Neville Hill 29/1/43.
Starbeck 29/11/47.

RENUMBERED:
2768 3/11/46.
62768 19/8/48.

CONDEMNED:
3/11/52.

366 THE OAKLEY

Darlington.

To traffic 7/12/34.

REPAIRS:
Dar. 1-21/2/35.**L.** *After collision.*
Dar. 1/4-30/5/36.**G.**
Dar. 10/11/37-19/1/38.**G.**
Dar. 4/7-12/8/39.**G.**
Dar. 25/2-28/3/41.**G.**
Dar. 22/9-27/10/42.**G.**
Dar. 10-30/7/43.**L.**
Cow. 23/8-23/9/44.**G.**
Cow. 11/5-1/6/46.**L.**
Dar. 12-24/10/46.**L.**
Ghd. 19-29/3/47.**L.**
Dar. 2/4-13/5/48.**G.**
Dar. 21-31/5/48.**N/C.**
Dar. 26/7-10/8/48.**N/C.**
Dar. 29/12/49-25/1/50.**G.**
Dar. 23/11-28/12/51.**G.**
Dar. 6/6/53.*Weigh.*
Dar. 24/9-23/10/53.**G.**
Dar. 2/2-5/3/56.**G.**
Dar. 12/9/58.*Not repaired.*

BOILERS:
2615.
2600 (*ex238*) 30/5/36.
2038 (*ex279*) 19/1/38.
2592 (*ex214*) 12/8/39.
2597 (*ex217*) 28/3/41.
2611 (*ex375*) 27/10/42.
2616 (*ex2749*) 13/5/48.
3788 (*ex2701*) 25/1/50.
27395 (*ex2770*) 28/12/51.
27435 (*new*) 23/10/53.
27371 (*ex2771*) 5/3/56.

SHEDS:
Gateshead.
Neville Hill 13/12/34.
York 5/2/40.
Neville Hill 28/2/40.
Scarborough 29/5/48.

RENUMBERED:
2769 24/10/46.
62769 13/5/48.

CONDEMNED:
12/9/58.

368 THE PUCKERIDGE

Darlington.

To traffic 12/12/34.

REPAIRS:
Dar. 13/9-16/10/35.**L.**
Dar. 1/9-22/10/36.**G.**
Dar. 18-26/2/37.**N/C.**
Dar. 12/5-7/7/38.**G.**

Dar. 22/11-23/12/39.**G.**
Dar. 23/7-5/9/41.**G.**
Dar. 14-26/8/42.**N/C.**
Cow. 24/9-16/10/43.**G.**
Cow. 29/9-24/11/45.**G.** *Rear sanding fitted.*
Ghd. 6-10/11/46.**L.**
Dar. 20/3-14/6/47.**L.**
Dar. 14/1-27/2/48.**G.**
Dar. 22/10-21/11/49.**G.**
Ghd. 24-27/11/49.**N/C.**
Dar. 7-29/11/51.**G.**
Dar. 6-12/12/51.**N/C.**
Dar. 5/3/53.*Weigh.*
Dar. 8/9/53-30/1/54.**G.**
Dar. 1-3/2/54.**N/C.**
Dar. 8-23/2/54.**N/C.**
Dar. 21/4-22/5/54.**C/L.**
Ghd. 16/1-15/2/57.**G.**

BOILERS:
2616.
2599 (*ex230*) 22/10/36.
2125 (*ex370*) 7/7/38.
2631 (*ex370*) 23/12/39.
2608 (*ex374*) 5/9/41.
2594 (*ex353*) 24/11/45.
2596 (*ex2763*) 27/2/48.
4002 (*new*) 21/11/49.
27380 (*ex2758*) 29/11/51.
27350 (*ex2713*) 15/2/57.

SHEDS:
Neville Hill.
Scarborough 27/7/48.
Selby 14/6/59.
York 13/9/59.

RENUMBERED:
2770 6/11/46.
E2770 27/2/48.
62770 21/11/49.

CONDEMNED:
23/9/59.

370 THE RUFFORD

Darlington.

To traffic 15/1/35.

REPAIRS:
Dar. 24/7-3/9/36.**G.**
Dar. 31/5-16/7/37.**N/C.**
Dar. 23/2-14/4/38.**G.**
Dar. 15-27/4/38.**N/C.**
Dar. 27/9-9/11/39.**G.**
Dar. 13/2-27/3/41.**L.** *After collision.*
Dar. 15/9-17/10/41.**G.**
Dar. 29/5-11/6/42.**N/C.**
Cow. 15/5-24/6/44.**G.**
Cow. 24/8-9/9/44.**L.**
Dar. 2/9-1/11/46.**G.**
Ghd. 31/3-22/4/48.**L.**

Dar. 1/7-16/8/49.**G.**
Ghd. 11-24/10/50.**N/C.**
Dar. 5/3-5/4/51.**G.**
Ghd. 15/4-10/5/52.**C/L.**
Ghd. 9-29/10/52.**C/L.**
Dar. 3/12/52-3/1/53.**H/I.**
Ghd. 11-14/11/53.**C/L.**
Ghd. 28/6-16/7/54.**N/C.**
Ghd. 2-26/5/55.**C/L.**
Ghd. 12/12/55-20/1/56.**G.**
Dar. 17/10/58. *Not repaired.*

BOILERS:
2626.
2125 (*ex352*) 3/9/36.
2631 (*ex374*) 14/4/38.
2615 (*ex363*) 9/11/39.
2596 (*ex364*) 17/10/41.
2599 (*ex364*) 24/6/44.
2654 (*ex256*) 1/11/46.
3815 (*ex2734*) 16/8/49.
27371 (*ex2703*) 5/4/51.
27827 (*new*) 20/1/56.

SHEDS:
Neville Hill.
Gateshead 31/1/42.
Blaydon 2/1/49.
York 10/6/56.

RENUMBERED:
2771 5/1/47.
62771 22/4/48.

CONDEMNED:
17/10/58.

374 THE SINNINGTON

Darlington.

To traffic 22/1/35.

REPAIRS:
Dar. 9/6-11/7/36.**G.**
Dar. 13-17/7/36.**N/C.**
Dar. 3/12/37-16/2/38.**G.**
Dar. 1-20/9/38.**N/C.**
Dar. 27/9-14/11/39.**G.**
Dar. 27/5-9/7/41.**G.**
Dar. 19/11-4/12/41.**L.**
Dar. 30/12/41-14/1/42.**L.**
Dar. 26/8-24/9/42.**L.**
Dar. 1/6-2/7/43.**G.**
Cow. 15/11-16/12/44.**G.**
Dar. 23/3-13/4/46.**L.**
Dar. 31/10-28/12/46.**G.**
Ghd. 18/2-10/3/48.**L.**
Dar. 2/12/48-15/2/49.**G.**
Dar. 27/11/50-27/1/51.**G.**
Dar. 24/9-25/10/52.**G.**
Dar. 4-6/11/52.**N/C.**
Dar. 4/2-14/5/55.**G.**
Dar. 16-20/5/55.**N/C.**
Dar. 24/9/58. *Not repaired.*

BOILERS:
2627.
2631 (*ex375*) 11/7/36.
2600 (*ex366*) 16/2/38.
2608 (*ex238*) 14/11/39.
2031 (*ex279*) 9/7/41.
2041 (*ex238*) 2/7/43.
7964 (*ex327*) 28/12/46.
2614 (*ex2737*) 15/2/49.
2614 Ren. 27363 27/1/51.
27429 (*new*) 25/10/52.

SHEDS:
Neville Hill.
Starbeck 4/1/48.
Neville Hill 3/6/56.
Selby 23/9/56.

RENUMBERED:
2772 28/12/46.
62772 15/2/49.

CONDEMNED:
24/9/58.

375 THE SOUTH DURHAM

Darlington.

To traffic 26/1/35.

REPAIRS:
Dar. 27/5-10/7/36.**G.**
Dar. 19/5-9/7/37.**H.**
Dar. 13-14/7/37.**N/C.**
Dar. 2/2-11/3/38.**G.**
Dar. 9-30/8/38. *Tender only.*
Dar. 1/3-17/4/39.**G.**
Dar. 17-21/4/39. *Brake exam.*
Dar. 30/9-2/11/40.**G.**
Dar. 17/8-19/9/42.**G.**
Cow. 15/5-8/7/44.**G.**
Cow. 2/3-6/4/46.**G.**
Dar. 28/1-5/3/48.**G.**
Dar. 11/1-22/2/50.**G.**
Dar. 30/4-12/5/51.**C/L.**
Dar. 16/11-13/12/51.**G.**
Dar. 20-24/12/51.**N/C.**
Dar. 18/1-13/2/54.**G.**
Dar. 15-18/2/54.**N/C.**
Dar. 11/1-9/2/56.**G.**
Dar. 5/8/58. *Not repaired.*

BOILERS:
2631.
2601 (*ex258*) 10/7/36.
127 (*ex205*) 17/4/39.
2611 (*ex232*) 2/11/40.
2606 (*ex361*) 19/9/42.
2154 (*ex1543*) 8/7/44.
2171 (*ex281*) 6/4/46.
2606 (*ex2774*) 5/3/48.
124 (*ex2774*) 22/2/50.
27394 (*ex2739*) 13/12/51.
27391 (*ex2747*) 13/2/54.
27829 (*new*) 9/2/56.

The eight Part 1 added in 1929 had the same coal and water capacities but were flush sided, that style having been made standard. 2757 DUMFRIES-SHIRE is at Eastfield shed. *T.G.Hepburn*

SHEDS:
Neville Hill.
Starbeck 8/12/47.
Neville Hill 23/6/57.

RENUMBERED:
 2773 10/11/46.
E2773 5/3/48.
62773 22/2/50.

CONDEMNED:
5/8/58.

376 THE STAINTONDALE

Darlington.

To traffic 2/2/35.

REPAIRS:
Dar. 11/2-20/3/36.**G.**
Dar. 27/9-5/11/37.**G.**
Dar. 22/3-9/5/39.**G.**
Dar. 13/11-13/12/40.**G.**
Dar. 16/12/40-17/1/41.**N/C.**
Dar. 28/12/42-3/2/43.**G.**
Cow. 13/9-14/10/44.**G.**
Cow. 6-27/10/45.**H.** *Rear sanding fitted.*
Ghd. 3-24/10/46.**L.**
Dar. 28/8-23/10/47.**G.**
Dar. 1/7-6/8/48.**L.**

Dar. 31/12/48-6/1/49.**L.**
Dar. 28/11-28/12/49.**G.**
Dar. 17/7-31/8/51.**G.**
Dar. 26-29/9/51.**N/C.**
Dar. 21-22/4/53.*Weigh*.
Dar. 21/12/53-20/3/54.**G.**
Dar. 22-23/3/54.**N/C.**
Dar. 17/5-20/6/56.**G.**
Dar. 13/11/58. *Not repaired*.

BOILERS:
 2632.
 2608 *(ex362)* 20/3/36.
 2014 *(ex329)* 5/11/37.
 7965 *(ex353)* 9/5/39.
 2000 *(ex336)* 13/12/40.
 1996 *(ex297)* 3/2/43.
 2606 *(ex375)* 14/10/44.
  124 *(ex2738)* 23/10/47.
 3809 *(ex2763)* 28/12/49.
27379 *(ex2752)* 31/8/51.
27388 *(ex2775)* 20/6/56.

SHEDS:
Neville Hill.
Scarborough 27/4/48.
Neville Hill 15/5/48.
Scarborough 15/8/48.
Pickering 26/9/48.
York 9/9/51.
Starbeck 5/12/54.
Neville Hill 16/6/57.

RENUMBERED:
 2774 27/10/46.
62774 6/8/48.

CONDEMNED:
13/11/58.

377 THE TYNEDALE

Darlington.

To traffic 11/2/35.

REPAIRS:
Dar. 4-21/10/35.**N/C.** *Prep.for test dept.*
Dar. 8/10-14/12/36.**G.**
Dar. 16-31/12/36.**N/C.**
Dar. 4-5/1/37.**N/C.**
Dar. 15/6-6/8/38.**G.**
Dar. 29/2-3/4/40.**G.**
Dar. 30/4-16/5/41.**N/C.**
Dar. 12/3-18/4/42.**G.**
Cow. 24/5-15/7/44.**G.**
Dar. 27/10-1/12/45.**L.**
Cow. 15/6-20/7/46.**H.**
Dar. 13/8-17/9/48.**G.**
Dar. 21/9-28/10/49.**C/L.**
Dar. 22-31/12/49.**C/L.**
Dar. 21/11-22/12/50.**G.**
Dar. 2-3/1/51.**N/C.**
Dar. 10-17/5/51.**C/L.** *New cam shaft fitted.*

Dar. 16/4-15/5/53.**G.**
Dar. 13/4-7/5/54.**C/L.**
Dar. 5-31/1/56.**G.**
Dar. 13-16/3/56.**N/C.**
Dar. 4/12/58. *Not repaired*.

BOILERS:
 2634.
 7952 *(ex255)* 6/8/38.
 7964 *(ex357)* 3/4/40.
 2044 *(ex211)* 18/4/42.
 2151 *(ex247)* 15/7/44.
 2611 *(ex2769)* 17/9/48.
27362 *(ex2704)* 22/12/50.
27388 *(ex2751)* 15/5/53.
27364 *(ex2763)* 31/1/56.

SHEDS:
Hull Botanic Gardens.
Neville Hill 31/5/39.
Selby 23/9/56.

RENUMBERED:
 2775 24/11/46.
62775 17/9/48.

CONDEMNED:
4/12/58.

The fifteen Part 2 built in 1932/33, and numbered in the range 201 to 298 did have new tenders included in the order for them, but there was a change of plan. The tenders actually built were the 3500 gallons flush sided type, but they were coupled with J38 class engines, whose existing tenders did not need that capacity, or the water pick-up apparatus with which they were fitted. Those stepped top tenders were delivered to Darlington who refurbished them, repainted them passenger green, and used them for the Part 2 engines they were building. They were to the same design as the Doncaster built tenders with Part 1, but as they had been built by Darlington in 1926 they did not have the redundant extra lamp iron.

The final 25 Part 2 engines added in 1934/35 had new flush sided 4200 gallons tender built with them at Darlington works. Twelve of them managed to keep their first tender through to withdrawal, and on another nine there was only interchanging of the same design. The other four, 2751, 2752, 2753 and 2756 are mentioned later. This view of 376 at York on 30th June 1935 shows that they had the vacuum brake cylinder on top of the tender at the right hand rear end. *L.Hanson*

In 1938 it became the turn of D49 class to be changed to less important tenders, so that theirs could be used to avoid the cost of building new ones for new engines of greater power. The five Part 3 in North Eastern Area, then being rebuilt to Part 1, had their Group Standard tenders taken for use by new V2 class, but as seven were needed, no.256 of Part 1, and no.336 of Part 2 were also changed. On those D49 class the replacement tender was the 4125 gallons N.E.R. coal rail type taken from Q6 class. *A.B.Crompton*

Six of the seven Q6 tenders put with D49 class were the type with coal rails dipped at both ends as seen with engine 327 NOTTING-HAMSHIRE, but as so often happened, there was an exception. The tender put with 318 CAMBRIDGESHIRE in 1938 had the rails cut off at the back of the coal space, and 318 (later 2720 and 62720) kept that tender to its October 1959 withdrawal. Like the other six, it was from Q6 class, actually no.2230. *P.H.Groom*

During the war the LNER obtained permission to build 25 class 02 mineral engines at Doncaster, on the proviso that second-hand tenders would be found for them to save steel for munitions. So the 4200 gallons Group Standard tenders still with 28 Part 1 engines were removed and replaced by surplus 4000 gallons type of Great Central design. Although they had stepped top they could be readily identified by their equally spaced axles, and different shape of slots in their framing as seen with 2756 SELKIRKSHIRE. *WBY collection*

Despite the replacement tenders for D49 class all having the same coal and water capacities, there were visible differences. Four of them had open coal rails when new and when altered to stop small coal slipping through, they had been plated *inside* the rails. Some were still fitted with water pick-up gear, the operating handwheel for which can be seen on 266's tender; Darlington removed that at their first opportunity. One with inside plated rails was withdrawn as late as April 1961 with 62716 KINCARDINESHIRE. *WBY collection*

365 - THE ODD ONE OUT.

(above) Ex Darlington on 24th January 1940, no.365 had been fitted with infinitely variable rotary cam poppet valve gear, and had a discernible difference. The cover to the end of the camshaft was smaller, and the driving rod was both longer and now outside the cylinder casing, instead of entering at the rear. *LNER*

(left) As altered, 365's poppet valves were controlled by steam pressure instead of by springs, but on the driver's side there was no indication that a change had been made. That steam control however "gave a fair amount of trouble" (to quote the Mechanical Engineer, Darlington) and so that arrangement was removed after 365 went into works on 27th February 1941. *LNER*

The war, and Gresley's death only five weeks later led to 365 being laid aside to await a decision as to its poppet valve gear. The new Chief Mechanical Engineer took the opportunity to try out another of his misguided ideas on standardisation, and caused fundamental change to be made to 365. When it did re-appear (after 18 months in works) it had two inside cylinders and piston valves, was changed from green to unlined black, but did have L N E R on tender, although by August 1942, only N E was being put on, and it was changed to that reduced version at its August 1944 general repair. *LNER*

When 365/2768 THE MORPETH was changed from Part 2 to Part 4, to serve its two inside cylinders and valves, a single 8-feed mechanical lubricator was enough, and its position was moved over to the right-hand running plate. *WBY collection*

In 1948/49 Darlington found it necessary to rebuild ten of the Great Central tenders coupled with D49 class. Frame and wheels were retained, but a flush sided tank was put on and the coping was moved from central to a more forward position. Some (but not all) were fitted with food and tool lockers at the front end. The water capacity on the rebuilds dropped from 4000 to 3800 gallons.

The other stepped top Great Central tenders continued to serve without rebuilding, this one with 62730 BERKSHIRE being at Leeds (City) station on a train to York after its 1950 transfer from Scottish to N.E.Region. At some time it had changed from G.C. to Group Standard buffer. *WBY collection*

As with boilers, it was found that to have a spare tender available enabled engines to be turned out more speedily from repairs, so in February 1947, Darlington seconded another Q6 tender to D49 class. 62756 THE BROCKLESBY had it until February 1953, when it was moved to 62751 THE ALBRIGHTON seen here at Darlington on 15th March 1959, two days after its withdrawal. For use with D49 class vacuum for train braking had to be added, and also a heater connection. In April 1949 to avoid delay caused by ex G.C. tenders being out of use for rebuilding, another Q6 tender was equipped for passenger working with D49 class. 62752 THE ATHERSTONE had it until August 1950, then 62749 THE COTTESMORE, and 62753 THE BELVOIR made use of it, but by April 1953 it was no longer needed. After standing spare for 5 1/2 years it was then sold for scrap. *WBY collection.*

Engines built to, and including no.329 had normal green lined painting with 7 1/2" L N E R, and 12" figures in shaded transfers on tender. As was Darlington's custom, the cylinder casing was also green, with lining panel, and on the buffer beam CLASS D49 in 2" was shown, but without Part differentiation in their LNER years. *Real Photos*

The 14 Part 1 in Scottish Area went to Cowlairs for their first general repair, and that works moved the number from tender to cab, but still kept 7½" L N E R on tender. They removed the classification from the buffer beam, but strangely (for that works) the cylinder casing kept its lined green, at least on 311 PEEBLES-SHIRE. *J.M.Craig*

By 1932 Cowlairs had come into line with the other works by putting 12" L N E R on tender, but were also then ceasing to apply green to the cylinder casing as shown by 265 LANARKSHIRE at Carlisle (Canal) shed on 11th August 1932. *L.Hanson*

Until after the war broke out in September 1939, 258 THE CATTISTOCK portrays D49 class as we were accustomed to see them, smart, even glossy, and it had *NOT* been painted or cleaned specially. *T.G.Hepburn*

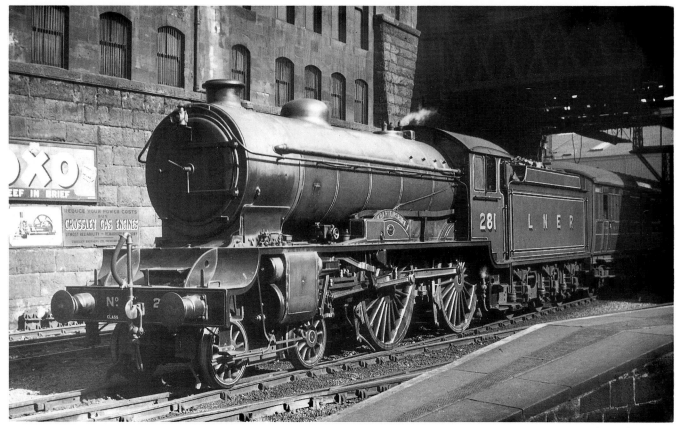

From 1932 to 1938 almost all maintenance was Darlington's responsibility, and when the Scottish Area engines went there, as 281 DUMBARTONSHIRE did for new cylinders in 1932, standard painting was applied, including that on cylinder casing. Here 281 is in Glasgow (Queen Street) about to return to Edinburgh. *WBY collection*

In November 1941 it was decided that, instead of green, black paint without any lining would have to suffice "for the duration". 318 out in the first week of 1942 was the official record for that change, and it was one of the restricted number to retain full L N E R on the tender. Note the cab windows have also been painted over to reduce glare from open firebox door as a contribution to Air Raid Precautions. *LNER*

From July 1942 there was further austerity in appearance, because L N E R was then reduced to only N E as seen on 2760 WESTMORLAND after it had been changed to Great Central tender and had a general repair at Cowlairs in August 1945. On 2nd September 1945, at Heaton Junction, Newcastle it is returning light engine to its home shed of Haymarket in Edinburgh. *WBY/AY*

2760 WESTMORLAND here at Eastfield shed in Glasgow is included to enable its pre-war appearance to be compared, and also to provide evidence that 2760 was a "Shire". *P.R.Wallis*

The 1946 general renumbering gathered all the D49s into the sequence 2700 to 2775, and on Sunday 17th November 1946 WESTMORLAND had been changed to 2735. So, on the next Sunday THE COTSWOLD was able to take 2760, which then was a Hunt instead of a Shire.

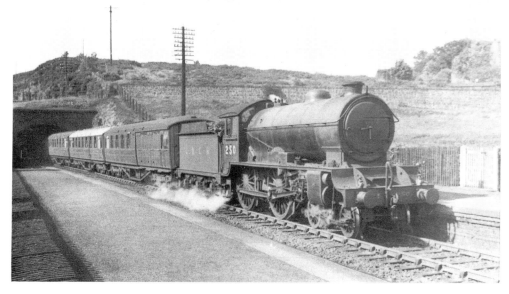

(*bottom*) In January 1946 it became possible to resume L N E R instead of only N E, and 250 PERTHSHIRE has it when working an express to Perth at North Queensferry, but this example shows the value, indeed necessity, of research based on primary sources. That engine's previous general repair (and any painting) was at Cowlairs in March 1945, when only N E was able to be used. But, at that repair it had a change of G.C. type tenders, and the one with which it came out had last been painted, and lettered L N E R, in January 1942 when Doncaster reconditioned it to send to Scottish Area where it was coupled to 266. That engine did have a general repair at Cowlairs in May 1944, but after only two years use its paint would get scant (if any) attention as a works well known for its cheeseparing attitude to paint renewal. So, LNER survived. *WBY collection*

61

2709 BERWICKSHIRE shows how D49 class ended their LNER years. It was ex Darlington in July 1947, when they had again taken over maintenance of all D49 class. Painting was unlined black, and with stocks of the expensive transfer applied figures and letters exhausted, 12" yellow painted and unshaded characters had become standard usage. They were supposed to be in Gill Sans, but due to an error in the February 1945 Doncaster drawing, figures 6 and 9 were the draughtsman's own interpretation of them, and erred by having a rounded tail to them. 2710 LINCOLNSHIRE was the last to have L N E R put on; it was ex works on 23rd January 1948. An interesting detail to note on 2709 is the bracket on the leading ring of the boiler, showing it was previously used on a Hunt class. *WBY collection*

The first British Railways style was applied to five, nos.2713, 2718, 2736, 2770 and 2773, which were ex works from 13th February to 19th March 1948. Still in unlined black, an E prefix denoted that they were Eastern & North Eastern Region stock, and only those five in D49 class acquired it. The cab had the usual 12" figures, but on the tender there was BRITISH RAILWAYS in 8" lettering. *H.C.Casserley*

Beginning with 62758 on 25th March 1948, running numbers were increased by 60,000, but at light repairs L N E R on tender was not disturbed, and by September, Darlington had so dealt with twelve. Gateshead works were also doing light repairs, and from 62753 out on 16th April 1948 to 62755 as late as 29th August 1949, they turned out twelve others. At those repairs, neither works fitted cast numberplate on smokebox door. Both first used 12" figures until September, but starting with 62714 ex Gateshead in October 1948, they had changed to 10". To avoid confusion with London Midland Region numbering, Carlisle (Canal) shed on Sunday 19th September 1948 added the 6 to their engines (2730, 2731, 2732, 2734 and 2735), but those five also kept L N E R on their tender. *E.Haigh collection*

At general repairs, 12" cab numbering was continued, but L N E R gave place to 8" BRITISH RAILWAYS, and five, nos.62762, 62749, 62705, 62769 and 62724 were so treated in April & May 1948. *A.B.Crompton*

British Railways announced its standard liveries in June 1948, and only rated D49 class as mixed traffic engines, so their black paint was continued but with red, cream, and grey lining added to it. 62751 here on 27th June, and still running in after a general repair was the first D49 to be so painted, and further changes had put the cab figures, and the tender lettering equally sized at 10" high. Note 62751's number was still carried on the buffer beam, with provision made on the smokebox door for fitting a cast numberplate, although *above* the upper hinge strap. A plate was duly fitted before 62751 was released to traffic on 6th July, but it was the only Part 1 or Part 2 to have it in that position. *B.V.Franey*

The next two to have general repair, 62765 out on the 2nd, and 62704 out on 9th July, did not have lining added, but did have matching figures and letters, and were also fitted with plate on smokebox door in what became the standard position. Note that, both on plate and on cab, the 6 with a tail was used.

Darlington went to the trouble of taking this official photograph of 62765 THE GOATHLAND when it was ex works from general repair on 31st May 1956, but for what purpose eluded both the late Ken Hoole and myself. We could not discern any difference from normal, but it does portray two items which could help pernickety modellers. The first smokebox numberplate which 62765 carried had wrong figure 6, and here a correct version has replaced it. The buffer beam also proves that Part classification *did* appear there. *LNER*

Ee! Who dun that? 62703 HERTFORDSHIRE fell into the turntable pit at Bridlington shed on 27th May 1958, and this view shows a lot of a D49 not normally seen. After its recovery it was sent to Darlington, but not surprisingly, that was the end of the road for it, because D49 class were by then on the withdrawal programme. *Hull Daily Mail*

62706 FORFARSHIRE, ex works 13th August 1948, was the first D49 to get correct Gill Sans 6 on cab, although the smokebox plate had already been cast showing them with tails; it proved to be the last in that style. *E.Haigh collection*

L N E R initials offered stout resistance to leaving D49 class, those put on 2725 INVERNESS-SHIRE when Darlington sent it out on 2nd January 1948 survived two light repairs, and the renumbering of the engine at one of them, to become the last D49 showing its original owners. That L N E R was seen until 62725 went into works on 5th October 1950, and so it never carried BRITISH RAILWAYS. *Real Photos*

Other 'freaks' could be seen in D49 class. In March 1950, an exchange of tenders coupled lined out 62752 with an unlined tender carrying BRITISH RAILWAYS. From 23rd August 1949 Darlington ceased applying that lettering because tenders were to have an emblem with lion-over-wheel. But transfers for it had not been delivered when 62714 (31st August), 62735 (2nd September), and 62722 (6th September) were released on completion of their repairs. Those three then ran with plain tender sides. *L.R.Peters*

(centre) Beginning on 21st September 1949 with 62758, all D49 class acquired the B.R. emblem on their lined black painting. It was handed for the lion to face forward on both sides of the tender, which was perfectly in order for an emblem, heraldic rules *not* being applicable to such free-lance designs. Three sizes of transfer were available, and on D49 class the largest (28") was always used. 62708 had emblem from a December 1949 repair. *A.B.Crompton*

*(below) I*n 1956, British Railways obtained a grant-of-arms, and then decided to use its crest instead of the emblem, but it was not until August 1957 that transfers for applying it became available. By June 1958, when D49 visits to Darlington paint shop ceased, eleven Part 1 and eight Part 2 had the emblem replaced by the crest. On 25th May 1958, no.62739 THE BADSWORTH was being used as station pilot at Scarborough. *K.Hoole*

Mention has already been made that 282 THE HURWORTH was originally fitted with an infinitely variable camshaft until March 1934 when that effort at improvement was discarded. This picture of 365 THE MORPETH is included to show that it was first fitted with the same set of seven fixed cams which had been made standard and to which 282 had been changed in 1934. *WBY collection*

The 1946 renumbering changed 365 to 2768, and after being in works (again) for over a year due to a fractured frame, on 19th August 1948 it came out as 62768, but still with L N E R on its tender, which it had regained in May 1947. Smokebox number plate had been fitted at its July 1950 general repair, the unique close spacing of the door straps causing it to be put above the upper one, and it also changed from L N E R directly to B.R. emblem. Note the buffer beam classification is D49/4, as seen here at Leeds on 23rd July 1950. *A.B.Crompton*

Early in October 1952, rough shunting at Starbeck shed caused this front end damage, and being very much of a singleton, repairs were not considered worth while, so it was withdrawn on 3rd November 1952. The boiler then served another five years on two Hunts, and the tender was used by another Hunt until July 1958. *J.W.Armstrong*

246 MORAYSHIRE had that name from new, although in the original list, Fifeshire had been entered against that number. Here at Eastfield shed in 1929, its original condition is shown for comparison with how it can still be seen. *J.M.Craig*

(centre) **MORAYSHIRE** as 62712 went to Hawick shed to do its final work, and on 10th March 1961 is in Carlisle station about to work back to Hawick on a stopping passenger train. This must be one of, if not the last, pictures showing a D49 on normal work, because at that date, only six (all Part 1) remained, and by May 2nd, only 62712 was left, and it was taken out of running stock on 3rd July 1961. *R.F.Orpwood*

(below) Very soon after it was seen in Carlisle, 62712 began to serve as a Stationary Boiler at Slateford Laundry in Edinburgh, where it was used until January 1962. Then for the next 2$\frac{1}{2}$ years it languished in store, which probably caused it to be overlooked for calling to Darlington for scrap. In July 1964 it was purchased privately for restoration to running condition, and the excellent job that Inverurie did is clearly to be seen when it was passing Arbroath on 5th January 1965. *Iain Wight*

(above) **There was a third effort at using infinitely variable gear with poppet valves. That from 365 was laid aside from 1941, and then re-appeared in February 1949 as here on 62764 THE GARTH but using spring - not steam - controlled valves.** *LNER*

(left) **On 30th April 1949, to acquire all these extra fittings, it left for the Rugby Testing Station; they were removed when it returned on 7th September 1949, but 62764 kept the infinitely variable valve gear until withdrawal on 13th November 1958, and results from it were not sufficiently good for any others to be fitted similarly.** *WBY collection*

J38 CLASS

1400

Darlington.

To traffic 28/1/26.

REPAIRS:
Cow. 15/7/32.**G.**
Cow. 16/3/34.**L.**
Cow. 2/1/36.**G.**
Cow. 11/7/36.**G.**
Cow. 18/10/38.**G.**
Cow. 5/12/38.**L.**
Cow. 20/1/39.**L.**
Cow. 21/9/40.**H.**
Cow. 12/10/40.**L.**
Cow. 18/4-5/6/42.**G.**
Cow. 1/12/42.**L.**
Cow. 4/6/43.**H.**
Cow. 2/6-28/7/45.**H.**
Cow. 9/5-5/7/47.**G.** *Screw Rev.fitted.*
Cow. 19/9-15/10/49.**H/I.**
Cow. 16/10-3/11/51.**G.**
Cow. 15-17/7/53.**N/C.**
Thj. 19-23/4/54.**C/L.**
Cow. 1/7-24/8/54.**H/I.**
Cow. 21/3-6/4/55.**C/L.**
Cow. 9/11-10/12/55.**C/H.**
Cow. 23/1-25/2/56.**C/H.**
Cow. 30/1-2/3/57.**H/I.**
Cow. 22/9-16/10/58.**H/I.**
Cow. 2/11-8/12/59.**C/L.**
Inv. 17/6-18/8/61.**G.**

BOILERS:
D1819 (C1427).
1437 *(ex1411)* 2/1/36.
1456 *(ex1442)* 11/7/36.
1439 *(ex1434)* 5/6/42.
1438 *(ex5923)* 5/7/47.
27603 *(ex5921)* 3/11/51.
27626 *(ex65909)* 10/12/55.
27583 *(ex64917)* 18/8/61.
Note - The original set of 35 boilers first carried Darlington registered numbers ranging from 1819 to 1866. Cowlairs Works discarded those, and put them into their register as 1427 to 1461; only those numbers were used subsequently.

SHEDS:
Dunfermline 5/2/26.
Thornton Junction 26/11/56.

RENUMBERED:
5900 8/9/46.
65900 15/10/49.

CONDEMNED:
25/11/63.
Cut up at Inverurie.

1401

Darlington.

To traffic 29/1/26.

REPAIRS:
Cow. 3-4/29.**G.**
Cow. 31/12/32.**G.**
Cow. 16/11/34.**G.**
Cow. 26/12/36.**G.**
Cow. 27/10/38.**G.**
Cow. 9/11/38.**N/C.**
Cow. 21/12/40-11/1/41.**G.**
Cow. 7/3/41.**L.**
Cow. 8/6/42.**L.**
Cow. 24/7/43.**H.**
Cow. 10/2-3/3/45.**H.** *Screw rev.fitted.*
Cow. 5-26/1/46.**L.**
Cow. 30/6-2/9/47.**G.**
Cow. 22/2-11/3/50.**H/I.**
Cow. 20/3-25/4/52.**G.**
Thj. 9-30/6/53.**C/L.**
Cow. 27/9-6/11/54.**L/I.**
Cow. 4-23/11/55.**H/I.**
Cow. 5-31/3/56.**H/I.**
Cow. 4-21/4/56.**C/L.**
Cow. 22-23/6/56.**C/L.**
Cow. 6-31/8/57.**C/L.**
Cow. 14/12/57-25/1/58.**G.**
Inv. 22/2-23/3/60.**H/I.**
Cow. 26/3-12/5/62.**G.**
Inv. 30/11/64-15/1/65.**H/I.**

BOILERS:
D1823 (C1428).
1438 *(ex1413)* 31/12/32.
1446 *(ex1426)* 26/12/36.
1448 *(ex1424)* 11/1/41.
1454 *(ex5912)* 2/9/47.
27480 *(ex65915)* 26/4/52.
27492 *(ex65930)* 25/1/58.
27582 *(ex65915)* 12/5/62.

SHED:
Thornton Junction 2/2/26.

RENUMBERED:
5901 8/9/46.
65901 11/3/50.

CONDEMNED:
22/4/67.
Sold for scrap to Motherwell Machinery & Scrap, Wishaw.

1403

Darlington.

To traffic 28/1/26.

REPAIRS:
Cow. 9-10/30.**G.**
Cow. 8/32-30/9/32.**G.**
Cow. 23/1/35.**H.**
Cow. 7/2/36.**G.**
Cow. 23/12/36.**H.**
Cow. 20/5/39.**G.**
Cow. 21/6/39.**L.**
Cow. 9/11/39.**L.**
Cow. 23/8-13/9/41.**G.**
Cow. 27/3/43.**H.**
Cow. 9/8/44.**L.**
Cow. 27/1-10/2/45.**G.** *Screw rev.fitted.*
Cow. 30/6-11/8/45.**L.**
Cow. 28/12/46-18/1/47.**L.**
Cow. 25/10/47-14/1/48.**G.**
Cow. 9/11-3/12/49.**L/I.**
Cow. 22/10-3/11/51.**L/I.**
StRx. 11-13/3/52.**C/L.**
Cow. 29/6-16/7/53.**G.**
Cow. 2-27/8/55.**H/I.**
Cow. 28/9-15/10/55.**C/L.**
Cow. 7/10-2/11/57.**G.**
Cow. 4-15/8/58.**C/L.**
Cow. 28/9-23/11/59.**L/I.**
Cow. 30/6-12/8/61.**L/I.**

BOILERS:
D1824 (C1429).
1442 *(ex1417)* 7/2/36.
1445 *(ex1446)* 13/9/41.
1445 Ren. 27614 3/11/51.
27619 *(ex65928)* 16/7/53.
27634 *(new)* 2/11/57.

SHEDS:
Dundee 28/1/26.
Thornton Junction 12/12/43.

RENUMBERED:
5902 19/5/46.
65902 3/12/49.

CONDEMNED:
28/12/63.
Sold for scrap to T.W.Ward, Inverkeithing.

1404

Darlington.

To traffic 30/1/26.

REPAIRS:
Dar. 23/3-13/5/31.**G.**
Dar. 22/5-6/7/33.**G.**
Cow. 18/3/35.**L.**
Cow. 16/11-2/12/35.**G.**
Cow. 1/11/36.**G.**
Cow. 15/7/37.**G.**
Cow. 20/9/37.**H.**
Cow. 13/9/40.**G.**
Cow. 18/4/42.**G.**
Cow. 12/6/43.**H.**
Cow. 11/11/44.**H.**
Cow. 1-21/9/45.**L.**
Cow. 3/10-6/11/46.**G.** *Screw rev.fitted.*
Cow. 7-21/6/47.**L.**
Cow. 3-25/2/50.**H/I.**
Cow. 14/4-17/5/52.**G.**
Inv. 26/1-25/2/55.**H/I.**
Inv. 18-23/11/55.**N/C.**
Cow. 7/12/55-7/1/56.**C/H.**
Cow. 1-23/2/57.**H/I.**
Cow. 28/2-2/3/57.**N/C.**
Cow. 7/4-1/5/59.**H/I.**
Cow. 12/6-14/7/61.**G.**
Cow. 3-26/1/63.**C/L.**
Cow. 4/8-23/10/65.**C/L.**
Cow. 26/5-18/6/66.**N/C.**

BOILERS:
D1826 (C1430).
1457 *(ex1443)* 2/12/35.
1458 *(ex1443)* 1/11/36.
1436 *(ex1442)* 18/4/42.
1802 *(ex5918)* 21/6/47.
27622 *(ex65901)* 17/5/52.
27485 *(ex64982)* 7/1/56.
27571 *(ex65927 & spare)* 14/7/61.

SHEDS:
Thornton Junction 30/1/26.
Dunfermline 30/1/61.

RENUMBERED:
5903 20/6/46.
65903 25/2/50.

CONDEMNED:
19/11/66.
Sold for scrap to Arnott Young, Old Kilpatrick.

1405

Darlington.

To traffic 29/1/26.

REPAIRS:
Dar. 3/3-24/4/31.**G.**
Cow. 26/10/34.**G.**
Cow. 18/4/36.**G.**
Cow. 19/3/38.**G.**
Cow. 20/3/39.**H.**
Cow. 29/11/41.**L.**
Cow. 24/10/42.**G.**
Cow. 9/9/44.**H.**
Cow. 24/5-21/6/46.**H/I.** *Screw rev.fitted.*
Cow. 26/1-26/2/49.**G.**
Cow. 14-15/3/49.**N/C.**

To provide a spare boiler so as to permit ready interchange on J38 class, in December 1932, no.1406 was fitted with a boiler as used by J39 class. To suit it, the J38 smokebox had to be 4' 8¾" long and the chimney was placed 6" further back. *H.C.Casserley*

65908 at Thornton shed on 17th May 1964 shows the 6" longer smokebox used with Diagram 97 boilers and the corresponding move of the chimney position. Its dome cover has an unusually flat top, but even with a rounded dome cover, all heights complied with the Composite Load Gauge so never needed any modifications. *P.H.Groom*

Cow. 28/8-23/9/50.**C/L.**
Cow. 25-26/10/50.**N/C.**
Cow. 23/1-16/2/52.**L/I.**
StRx. 12-19/3/52.**N/C.**
Cow. 26/2-7/3/53.**C/L.**
Cow. 3-26/3/55.**G.**
Cow. 13/5-13/6/57.**H/I.**
Cow. 18-22/3/58.**C/L.**
Cow. 9-12/2/59.**N/C.**
Cow. 5-20/6/59.**G.**
Thj. 17/8-16/9/60.**C/L.**
Cow. 13-31/3/62.**L/I.**

BOILERS:
D1828 (C1431).
  1443 *(ex1426)* 26/10/34.
  1429 *(ex1403)* 18/4/36.
  1450 *(ex1427)* 19/3/38.
  1456 *(ex1400)* 24/10/42.
  1461 *(ex5932)* 26/2/49.
  1461 Ren. 27627 16/2/52.
  27623 *(ex65926)* 26/3/55.
  27825 *(ex62756 and Spare)* 20/6/
  59.

SHEDS:
Dundee 29/1/26.
Thornton Junction 12/12/43.

RENUMBERED:
5904 25/8/46.
65904 26/2/49.

CONDEMNED:
23/7/64.
*Sold for scrap to Arnott Young,
Old Kirpatrick.*

1406

Darlington.

To traffic 30/1/26.

REPAIRS:
Dar. 4/3-19/5/31.**G.**
Cow. 20/9-5/12/32.**G.**
Cow. 26/9/34.**G.**
Cow. 15/7/37.**H.**
Cow. 2/8/37.**L.**
Cow. 18/11-2/12/39.**G.**
Cow. 8/11-13/12/41.**G.**
Cow. 26/6/43.**L.**
Cow. 3/7/44.**L.**
Cow. 26/10/44.**L.**
Cow. 22/4/45.**H.**
Cow. 2-15/6/45.**L.**
Inv. 4/5-5/10/46.**G.**
Cow. 26/5-18/6/48.**H/I.** *Screw
rev.fitted.*
Cow. 5-30/12/50.**G.**
Cow. 16/3-18/4/51.**C/L.**
Cow. 6/2-15/3/52.**L/I.**
Cow. 6/10-13/11/54.**G.**
Cow. 30/5-29/6/57.**H/I.**
Cow. 27/4-16/5/59.**G.**
Cow. 5-6/6/59.**N/C.**

Inv. 7/4-4/5/62.**H/I.**
Inv. 17-18/5/62.**N/C.**
Inv. 27/12/63-3/1/64.**N/C.**
Inv. 7/10-13/11/64.**L/I.**

BOILERS:
D1829 (C1432).
  1800 *(new)* 5/12/32.
  1453 *(ex1441)* 2/12/39.
  1442 *(ex1403)* 13/12/41.
  1458 *(ex1447)* 5/10/46.
  2029 *(new)* 30/12/50.
  2029 Ren. 27579 15/3/52.
  27529 *(ex65907)* 13/11/54.
  27418 *(ex62702)* 16/5/59.

SHEDS:
Dunfermline 8/2/26.
Thornton Junction 26/11/56.

RENUMBERED:
5905 27/10/46.
65905 18/6/48.

CONDEMNED:
25/5/66.
*Sold for scrap to Shipbreaking
Industries, Faslane.*

1407

Darlington.

To traffic 13/2/26.

REPAIRS:
Dar. 27/11/31-14/1/32.**G.** *New
tender.*
Cow. 3/3-17/4/34.**G.**
Cow. 16/5-12/6/36.**G.**
Cow. 22/10/37.**L.**
Cow. 11/5/38.**G.**
Cow. 5/7/40.**H.**
Cow. 14/6/41.**G.**
Cow. 22/6/43.**L.**
Cow. 11/3/44.**H.**
Cow. 17/3-7/4/45.**L.**
Cow. 1/5-2/7/47.**H/I.** *New
cylinders. Screw rev.fitted.*
Cow. 23/3-13/4/50.**H/I.**
Cow. 23-27/4/51.**C/L.**
Cow. 14/10-8/11/52.**G.**
Cow. 23/11-18/12/53.**C/L.**
Cow. 25/11/55-21/1/56.**L/I.**
Cow. 2-4/5/57.**N/C.**
Cow. 26/7-31/8/57.**G.**
Cow. 7/8-10/9/59.**L/I.**
Thj. 12-26/2/62.**C/L.**
Cow. 7/5-15/6/62.**G.**

BOILERS:
D1830 (C1433).
  1447 *(ex1423)* 17/4/34.
  1433 *(ex1428)* 12/6/36.
  1709 *(ex1415)* 14/6/41.
  135 *(ex4849)* 2/7/47.
  27608 *(ex65900)* 8/11/52.

27509 *(ex64892)* 31/8/57.
27579 *(ex65919)* 15/6/62.

SHEDS:
St Margarets 13/2/26.
Haymarket 9/40.
St Margarets 17/3/44.
Dunfermline 18/4/61.

RENUMBERED:
5906 3/11/46.
65906 13/4/50.

CONDEMNED:
6/8/65.
*Sold for scrap to Motherwell
Machinery & Scrap, Wishaw.*

1408

Darlington.

To traffic 3/3/26.

REPAIRS:
Cow. 1/28.**G.**
Cow. 7/10/33.**G.**
Cow. 16/5/36.**H.**
Cow. 6/1/38.**H.**
Cow. 28/6/39.**L.**
Cow. 2/12/39.**G.**
Cow. 7/6-9/8/41.**H.**
Cow. 27/3/43.**H.**
Cow. 8/4/43.**L.**
Cow. 31/3/45.**G.** *Screw Rev. fitted.*
Cow. 4/9/45.**L.**
Cow. 14/9/46.**L.**
Cow. 20/11-7/12/46.**H/I.**
Cow. 6-31/12/48.**G.**
Cow. 5/5/49.**N/C.**
Cow. 29/9/49.**C/L.**
Cow. 10/12/49.**C/L.**
Thj. 21/7/50.**C/L.**
Cow. 17/9-12/10/51.**L/I.**
Cow. 7/7-8/8/53.**C/L.**
Cow. 9/6-17/7/54.**G.**
Inv. 9/5-8/6/56.**L/I.**
Cow. 2/7-9/8/58.**G.**
Cow. 12/11-3/12/60.**L/I.**
Cow. 21/3-20/4/63.**G.**

BOILERS:
D1831 (C1434).
  1432 *(ex1437)* 2/12/39.
  1434 *(ex1440)* 31/3/45.
  144 *(ex5914)* 31/12/48.
  144 Ren. 27529 12/10/51.
  27535 *(ex64930)* 17/7/54.
  27614 *(ex65932)* 9/8/58.
  27510 *(ex65934)* 20/4/63.

SHED:
Thornton Junction.

RENUMBERED:
5907 22/9/46.
65907 31/12/48.

CONDEMNED:
22/8/66.
*Sold for scrap to Motherwell
Machinery & Scrap, Wishaw.*

1409

Darlington.

To traffic 24/2/26.

REPAIRS:
Dar. 10/5-13/6/32.**G.** *New tender.*
Cow. 25/2/34.**G.**
Cow. 25/6-11/7/36.**G.**
Cow. 15/9/38.**H.**
Cow. 2/3/40.**L.**
Cow. 5/4/41.**G.**
Cow. 9/5/42.**L.**
Cow. 24/4/43.**H.**
Cow. 3-24/2/45.**G.** *Screw
rev.fitted.*
Cow. 6-13/4/46.**L.**
Cow. 29/8-20/9/47.**H/I.**
Cow. 20/12/49-14/1/50.**G.**
Cow. 2-14/4/51.**N/C.**
Cow. 23/9-11/10/52.**L/I.**
Thj. 12-22/4/54.**C/L.**
Cow. 10/5-2/6/54.**N/C.**
Cow. 1/7-13/8/55.**G.**
Cow. 22-27/8/55.**N/C.**
Thj. 24/10-21/11/56.**C/L.**
Cow. 2/4-5/5/57.**H/I.**
Cow. 2-24/10/58.**L/I.**
Inv. 24/1-3/3/61.**G.**
Thj. 12/12/61-17/1/62.**C/L.**
Inv. 15/7-23/8/63.**L/I.**

BOILERS:
D1833 (C1435).
  1441 *(ex1416)* 11/7/36.
  1446 *(ex1401)* 5/4/41.
  1803 *(ex1437)* 24/2/45.
  1449 *(ex5926)* 14/1/50.
  1449 Ren. 27618 11/10/52.
  27573 *(ex64917)* 13/8/55.
  27702 *(ex65910)* 3/3/61.

SHED:
Thornton Junction 2/3/26.

RENUMBERED:
5908 6/10/46.
65908 14/1/50.

CONDEMNED:
17/9/64.
*Sold for scrap to Motherwell
Machinery & Scrap, Wishaw.*

1410

Darlington.

To traffic 15/2/26.

The Darlington type steam reversing gear was only changed to screw operated from 1945 to 1948, and many only got it after they had been renumbered during 1946 into the 5900 to 5934 series. The long sloping rod instead of the small diameter pipe indicated that change, and this view also shows that the top lamp iron is of Group Standard pattern mounted *on* the smokebox door, which had superseded the Darlington mounting position above the smokebox, as built. Cowlairs began to make that change from 1935. *J.L.Stevenson*

REPAIRS:
Cow. 16/3/33.**G.**
Cow. 9/11/34.**L.**
Cow. 4/7/35.**H.**
Cow. 24/3/37.**H.**
Cow. 11/8/37.**L.**
Cow. 24/2/39.**G.**
Cow. 16/11/39.**L.**
Cow. 5/4/41.**G.**
Cow. 11/10/41.**L.**
Cow. 19/6/42.**L.**
Cow. 15/5/43.**H.**
Cow. 24/3-14/4/45.**G.** *Screw rev. fitted.*
Cow. 1-15/12/45.**L.**
Cow. 28/7-18/9/47.**G.**
Cow. 31/10-26/11/49.**L/I.**
Cow. 14/9-20/10/51.**G.**
Efd. 29/1-13/2/52.**C/L.**
Cow. 1/4-2/5/53.**L/I.**
Cow. 19-21/5/53.**N/C.**
Pol. 8/9-28/10/54.**C/L.**
Cow. 10/10-5/11/55.**G.**
Cow. 11/6-5/7/58.**L/I.**
Inv. 13/7-2/9/60.**G.** *A.W.S.fitted.*
Inv. 11/10-1/12/60.**N/C.**
Cow. 19/11-8/12/62.**G.**
Cow. 5/2-6/3/64.**C/L.**
Inv. 9/9-9/10/65.**C/L.**
Inv. 18-26/11/65.**N/C.**

BOILERS:
D1835 (C1436).

1803 *(new)* 4/7/35.
1457 *(ex1445)* 5/4/41.
27626 *(ex5934)* 20/10/51.
27651 *(ex64971)* 5/11/55.
27822 *(ex65909)* 2/9/60.
27589 *(ex65934)* 8/12/62.

SHEDS:
Dunfermline 15/2/26.
Polmont 15/5/49.
Grangemouth 18/5/64.
Thornton Junction 1/8/64.

RENUMBERED:
5909 27/7/46.
65909 26/11/49.

CONDEMNED:
19/11/66.
Sold for scrap to Arnott Young, Old Kilpatrick.

1411

Darlington.

To traffic 3/3/26.

REPAIRS:
Cow. 1-2/31.**G.**

Cow. 3/33.**G.**
Cow. 1/12/34.**H.**
Cow. 11/35-2/12/35.**G.**
Cow. 19/5/37.**G.**
Cow. 23/10/37.**L.**
Cow. 23/12/39.**G.**
Cow. 11/1-22/3/41.**G.**
Cow. 7/11/41.**L.**
Cow. 24/7/42.**L.**
Cow. 4/9/43.**H.**
Cow. 6-30/11/45.**G.** *Screw rev.fitted.*
Cow. 6/7-14/8/48.**H/I.**
Cow. 25/4-20/5/50.**G.**
Efd. 27/11-15/12/51.**C/L.**
Thj. 11-12/1/52.**C/L.**
Cow. 17/8-14/9/53.**H/I.**
Cow. 14-28/4/56.**G.**
Cow. 7-19/5/56.**C/L.**
Cow. 29/8-25/9/58.**H/I.**
Inv. 27/8-14/10/60.**G.** *A.W.S.fitted.*
Inv. 4-12/1/61.**N/C.**
Inv. 10/10-13/11/62.**L/I.**
Inv. 15-20/11/62.**N/C.**
Inv. 2-6/3/65.**N/C.**

BOILERS:
D1836 (C1437).
1454 *(ex1440)* 2/12/35.
1460 *(ex1440)* 22/3/41.
1429 *(ex1444)* 30/11/45.
2017 *(new)* 20/5/50.

2017 Ren. 27569 14/9/53.
27702 *(ex64809)* 28/4/56.
27452 *(ex64853)* 14/10/60.

SHEDS:
Dundee 3/3/26.
Thornton Junction 12/12/43.

RENUMBERED:
5910 14/9/46.
65910 14/8/48.

CONDEMNED:
14/7/66.
Sold for scrap to Geo.H.Campbell, Airdrie.

1413

Darlington.

To traffic 3/3/26.
REPAIRS:
Cow. 12/7-14/9/30.**G.**
Cow. 3/12/32.**G.**
Cow. 17/6/33.**G.**
Cow. 6/33-9/9/33.**H.**
Cow. 3-5/35. **H.**
Cow. 23/4/36.**H.**
Cow. 12/5/38.**H.**
Cow. 20/6/38.**N/C.**
Cow. 7-28/12/40.**G.**

Dar. 29/3/41.**L.**
Dar. 1/8/41.**L.**
Dar. 2/12/41-16/1/42.**L.** *Left piston rod bent.*
Cow. 21/10/42.**H.**
Cow. 24/3-14/4/45.**H/I.** *Screw rev.fitted.*
Cow. 30/8-21/9/46.**G.**
Cow. 23-30/11/46.**L.**
Cow. 16/12/48-21/1/49.**H/I.**
Cow. 1/5-7/6/52.**G.**
Cow. 11-20/6/52.**N/C.**
Cow. 9-11/10/52.**N/C.**
Thj. 30/12/53-13/1/54.**C/L.**
Cow. 2-31/12/54.**L/I.**
Cow. 31/8-13/10/56.**L/I.**
Cow. 19/3-26/4/58.**G.**
Inv. 2/4-20/5/60.**H/I.**
Inv. 30-31/5/60.**N/C.**
Cow. 23/11-15/12/62.**G.**
Cow. 17/2-5/3/66.**C/L.**
Cow. 18-27/4/66.**N/C.**

BOILERS:
D1837 (C1438).
  1432 *(ex1406)* 3/12/32.
  1428 *(ex1401)* 17/6/33.
  1432 *(ex1413)* 9/9/33.
  1802 *(new)* 5/35.
  1451 *(ex1416)* 28/12/40.
  1446 *(ex1409)* 14/4/45.
  1428 *(ex5914)* 21/9/46.
  27453 *(ex64778)* 7/6/52.
  27588 *(ex64929)* 26/4/58.
  27822 *(ex65909)* 15/12/62.

SHED:
Thornton Junction 3/3/26.

RENUMBERED:
5911 10/11/46.
65911 21/1/49.

CONDEMNED:
1/3/67.
Sold for scrap to Motherwell Machinery & Scrap, Wishaw.

Until late in 1931 all had this tender type with stepped top, but by December 1933 had been changed to smaller capacity flush sided type. As goods engines they were first fitted with plain 3-link front coupling as seen here, but all were subsequently changed to the screw adjustable type.

When this class was built in 1926, it was Darlington custom not to fit a standpipe for the vacuum brake connection at the front end, a hose on a union under the buffer beam serving that purpose. Curiously they also fitted J38 engines with Spencer double-case buffers, the same type as used by the Pacifics, although both D49 and J39 classes got Group Standard pattern. The Spencer buffers had a spring in front of the beam, and another behind it, the beam having to be drilled to take the spindle. The arrangement for operating the drop grate should be noted as that was changed later.

Here at Craigentinny on 8th August 1932 with the smaller tender, 1414 has been fitted with swan-neck standpipe for the front vacuum brake connection which Darlington had adopted as standard from 1929 as part of the Unification of Brakes Programme. *J.T.Rutherford*

76

On the replacement boilers the whistle was above an isolating valve mounted on a pad fitted on the firebox. That cured the previous tendency of the pipe to break inside the cab causing danger to the crew. In due course, the older boilers were changed to that improved style, 1443 having the benefit of that alteration. Note that it still retains circular cover around the base of the safety valves. *T.G.Hepburn*

Starting sometime during the 1939-45 war, Cowlairs tended to discard the cover to the safety valves. 1417 was so bereft when ex works on 29th June 1946, but at that repair its tender had regained full L N E R lettering instead of the wartime N E only. This view also shows the modification made to the drop grate operating gear. *WBY collection*

1414

Darlington.

To traffic 2/3/26.

REPAIRS:
Cow. 11/30.**G.**
Dar. 21/12/31-8/2/32.**G.**
Cow. 14/8/34.**G.**
Cow. 15/8-5/9/36.**G.**
Cow. 11/11/38.**G.**
Cow. 17/12/38.**L.**
Cow. 6/7/39.**L.**
Cow. 1/6/40.**L.**
Cow. 14/6/41.**G.**
Cow. 12/9/41.**L.**
Cow. 17/4/43.**H.**
Cow. 11/11/44.**H.**
Cow. 9/7-20/9/47.**G.** *Screw rev.fitted.*
Cow. 18/11-9/12/49.**H/I.**
Cow. 10/7-16/8/52.**G.**
Cow. 27/11-26/12/53.**H/I.**
Cow. 23/12/55-11/2/56.**H/I.**
Cow. 24/3-3/5/58.**G.**
Cow. 30/3-17/4/59.**N/C.**
Cow. 10-23/2/60.**N/C.**
Inv. 14/10-2/12/60.**H/I.**
A.W.S.fitted.
Inv. 28/3-6/4/61.**N/C.**
Cow. 12/2-23/3/63.**G.**
Cow. 28-30/3/63.**N/C.**
Inv. 7-14/10/65.**C/L.**
Cow. 13/6-9/7/66.**C/L.**

BOILERS:
D1838 (C1439).
  1435 *(ex1409)* 5/9/36.
  1454 *(ex1411)* 14/6/41.
  1448 *(ex5901)* 20/9/47.
  27499 *(ex65903)* 16/8/52.
  27506 *(ex64930)* 3/5/58.
  27591 *(ex65925)* 23/3/63.

SHEDS:
St Margarets 2/3/26.
Dalry Road 12/10/64.
Dunfermline 7/3/65.

RENUMBERED:
  5912 8/9/46.
  65912 9/12/49.

CONDEMNED:
19/11/66.
Sold for scrap to Arnott Young, Old Kilpatrick.

1415

Darlington.

To traffic 2/3/26.

REPAIRS:
Cow. 9-10/30.**G.**
Cow. 27/2/32.**G.**
Cow. 30/1/34.**G.**
Cow. 28/9-5/10/35.**G.**
Cow. 31/8/37.**H.**
Cow. 28/9/38.**L.**
Cow. 2/9/39.**G.**
Cow. 17-31/5/41.**G.**
Cow. 12/6/43.**H.**
Cow. 19/10-8/11/45.**G.** *Screw rev.fitted.*
Cow. 5-19/4/47.**L.**
Cow. 10/3-10/7/48.**H/I.** *New cyls.*
Cow. 10/8-2/9/49.**G.**
Cow. 12/2-14/3/52.**G.**
Cow. 29/10-20/11/54.**H/I.**
Cow. 17/6-13/7/57.**G.**
Cow. 31/12/58-24/1/59.**H/I.**
Cow. 15-16/9/59.**N/C.**
Cow. 1-30/6/61.**G.**
Cow. 1-4/11/61.**N/C.**
Cow. 11/2-9/3/63.**H/I.**

BOILERS:
D1839 (C1440).
  1709 *(ex2731)* 5/10/35.
  1441 *(ex1409)* 31/5/41.
  1444 *(ex1443)* 10/7/48.
  27466 *(ex5927)* 14/3/52.

27517 *(ex64895)* 13/7/57.
27524 *(ex64848)* 30/6/61.

SHED:
Thornton Junction 5/3/26.

RENUMBERED:
  5913 27/10/46.
  65913 10/7/48.

CONDEMNED:
6/8/64.
Cut up at Cowlairs.

1416

Darlington.

To traffic 18/3/26.

REPAIRS:
Cow. 10-12/30.**G.**
Cow. 10/12/34.**G.**
Cow. 16/5/36.**G.**
Cow. 13/2/37.**H.**
Cow. 23/6/35.**L.**
Cow. 18/2/39.**G.**
Cow. 10/4/40.**L.**
Cow. 25/5-11/6/40.**G.**
Cow. 27/12/41.**H.**
Inv. 10/12/42.**L.**
Cow. 20/5/44.**H.**
Cow. 14-21/7/45.**L.**
Cow. 15/12/45-12/1/46.**L.**
Cow. 15/9-12/10/46.**G.** *Screw rev.fitted.*
Cow. 30/6-4/8/48.**G.**
Cow. 28/9-28/10/50.**H/I.**
Cow. 1-10/2/51.**C/L.**
Cow. 10/3-2/5/53.**G.**
Cow. 3-10/6/54.**N/C.**
Cow. 19/8-10/9/55.**L/I.**
Cow. 8/11-8/12/56.**C/L.**
Cow. 27/2-30/3/57.**G.**
Cow. 6-26/6/59.**H/I.**

Cow. 13-26/1/61.**N/C.**
Cow. 26/1-10/3/62.**G.**
Cow. 15-21/11/62.**N/C.**
Inv. 1/6-21/8/65.**H/I.**

BOILERS:
D1840 (C1441).
  1451 *(ex1422)* 16/5/36.
  1428 *(ex1419)* 11/6/40.
  144 *(ex4917)* 12/10/46.
  2938 *(ex4925)* 4/8/48.
  27624 *(ex65909)* 2/5/53.
  27610 *(ex65931)* 30/3/57.
  27569 *(ex65923)* 10/3/62.

SHEDS:
St Margarets 24/4/26.
Thornton Junction 15/11/64.

RENUMBERED:
  5914 1/9/46.
  65914 4/8/48.

CONDEMNED:
19/11/66.
Sold for scrap to Arnott Young, Old Kilpatrick.

1417

Darlington.

To traffic 20/3/26.

REPAIRS:
Dar. 27/11/31-15/1/32.**G.**
Cow. 14/9-5/10/35.**G.**
Cow. 26/7/37.**H.**
Cow. 12/5/39.**L.**
Cow. 18/8/39.**L.**
Cow. 1/6/40.**G.**
Dar. 22/12/41-19/3/42.**G.**
Dar. 20/3-16/6/42.**H.**
Cow. 29/10/42.**L.**
Cow. 19/8/44.**G.**

From new, all had the facility of being able to drop the front part of the grate to assist clearance of ash and clinker, and the inclined operating rod worked a crank under the semi-circular cover on the running plate. Later, the rod was more steeply inclined, which enabled the cover on the running plate to be removed. *WBY collection*

From 1933 until 1959 all were coupled with the same design of 3500 gallons tender, but then two variants were introduced. Ex Inverurie works in May 1960 no.65911 took out - and then retained - a 3500 gallons tender which had been built in 1938 for class K4; it was of the high front plate type which by then, had become standard. The other tender variant stemmed from 65902 being called to Cowlairs in February 1959 because the tender coupled with it since February 1932 had been condemned for scrapping. The replacement gave 65902 a reversion to 4200 gallons capacity, and a useless scoop. It was a flush sided tender which K3 class 2769/61898 had used from new in February 1930 until that engine was withdrawn in February 1959. Then, in September 1961 a similar change took place with 65919, whose replacement had come from withdrawn K3 class no. 1162/61916. At sometime in the 1950's that tender's backplate to the coal space had been made higher and moved forward, as can be seen here at Dundee in February 1964. *J.L.Stevenson*

Cow. 16-30/6/45.**L.**
Cow. 29/9-6/10/45.**L.**
Cow. 1-29/6/46.**H/I.** *Screw rev.fitted.*
Cow. 8-25/9/48.**H/I.**
Cow. 12/6/50-20/1/51.**L/I.**
Cow. 24/5-23/6/51.**G.**
Thj. 4/6-4/7/52.**N/C.**
Cow. 13/2/53.**N/C.**
Cow. 5/10-7/11/53.**H/I.**
Cow. 8/6-14/7/56.**G.**
Cow. 21/6-19/7/58.**H/I.**
Cow. 19/6-19/8/61.**G.**
Cow. 11/7-18/8/62.**C/H.**
Inv. 23/8-2/9/65.**N/C.**

BOILERS:
D1843 (C1442).
 1449 *(ex1437)* 5/10/35.
 1800 *(ex1420)* 19/8/44.
 2031 *(new)* 20/1/51.
 2031 Ren. 27580 7/11/53.
 27582 *(ex65933)* 14/7/56.
 27482 *(ex64934)* 19/8/61.
 27581 *(ex65920)* 18/8/62.

SHEDS:
St Margarets 26/3/26.
Thornton Junction 4/4/65.

RENUMBERED:
 5915 14/9/46.
 65915 25/9/48.

CONDEMNED:
19/11/66.
Sold for scrap to Arnott Young, Old Kilpatrick.

1419

Darlington.

To traffic 13/3/26.

REPAIRS:
Cow. 4/11/33.**G.**
Cow. 26/10/35.**H.**
Cow. 5/7/38.**H.**
Cow. 11/11/38.**H.**
Cow. 10/6/39.**N/C.**

Cow. 2/12/39.**G.**
Cow. 15/6/40.**L.**
Cow. 5-19/4/41.**G.**
Cow. 7/3/42.**H.**
Cow. 25/9/43.**H.**
Cow. 30/10-17/11/45.**G.** *Screw rev.fitted.*
Cow. 30/12/46-31/1/47.**G.**
Cow. 6-20/12/47.**L.**
Cow. 13/4-13/5/49.**H/I.**
Cow. 24/5-23/6/51.**G.**
Thj. 4/6-4/7/52.**C/L.**
Cow. 13/2/53.**N/C.**
Cow. 20/8-19/9/53.**H/I.**
Cow. 15-24/10/53.**N/C.**
Cow. 14/2-17/3/56.**G.**
Cow. 5/4-4/5/57.**C/L.**
Cow. 15/1-22/2/58.**H/I.**
Inv. 29/8-18/11/60.**G.**
A.W.S.fitted.
Inv. 22/8-8/9/61.**N/C.**
Cow. 8/3-6/4/63.**L/I.**
Inv. 11/12/63-3/1/64.**N/C.**

BOILERS:
D1844 (C1443).

1428 *(ex1413)* 4/11/33.
1431 *(ex1423)* 2/12/39.
1430 *(ex1421)* 19/4/41.
1433 *(ex5929)* 31/1/47.
27601 *(ex5910)* 23/6/51.
27603 *(ex65900)* 17/3/56.
27548 *(ex65922)* 18/11/60.

SHEDS:
Dunfermline 26/3/26.
St Margarets 10/11/54.
Thornton Junction 18/4/61.

RENUMBERED:
 5916 27/7/46.
 65916 13/5/49.

CONDEMNED:
30/10/65.
Sold for scrap to J.McWilliam, Shettleston.

1420

Darlington.

To traffic 18/3/26.

REPAIRS:
Dar. 16/6-11/8/31.**G.**
Cow. 10/8/35.**G.**
Cow. 22/2/36.**G.**
Cow. 6/9/37.**H.**
Cow. 20/5/39.**L.**
Cow. 20/4/40.**G.**
Cow. 12/9/42.**H.**
Cow. 6/5/44.**G.**
Cow. 3/3-11/4/46.**G.** *Screw rev.fitted.*
Cow. 18/3-7/5/48.**G.**
Cow. 18/9-20/10/50.**G.**
Cow. 4/11/52-10/1/53.**G.**
Pol. 9/2-16/3/54.**C/L.**
Cow. 31/5-5/6/54.**N/C.**
Inv. 9/2-25/3/55.**L/I.**
Inv. 14-27/5/55.**N/C.**
Cow. 23-26/11/55.**N/C.**
Cow. 8/3-7/4/56.**H/I.**
Cow. 20/9-4/10/56.**C/L.**
Cow. 11-13/7/57.**N/C.**
Cow. 26/12/57-1/2/58.**G.**
Inv. 21/10-16/12/60.**L/I.**
A.W.S.fitted.
Cow. 19/4-26/5/62.**C/H.**
Cow. 27/3-27/4/63.**G.**

BOILERS:
D1845 (C1444).
1436 *(ex1410)* 10/8/35.
1455 *(ex1441)* 22/2/36.
1800 *(ex1406)* 20/4/40.
1437 *(ex1427)* 6/5/44.
1441 *(ex5913)* 7/5/48.
27561 *(ex64927)* 10/1/53.
27604 *(ex65925)* 1/2/58.
25831 *(ex64945)* 27/4/63.

SHEDS:
Dunfermline.
Polmont 15/5/49.
Grangemouth 18/5/64.
Thornton Junction 1/8/64.
Dunfermline 31/8/64.

RENUMBERED:
5917 8/9/46.
65917 7/5/48.

CONDEMNED:
19/11/66.
Sold for scrap to Arnott Young, Old Kilpatrick.

1421

Darlington.

To traffic 18/3/26.

REPAIRS:
Dar. 6/3-21/5/31.**G.**
Cow. 14/5/32.**L.**
Cow. 10/33-16/11/33.**G.**
Cow. 4/1/36.**G.**
Cow. 21/10/37.**H.**
Cow. 1/7/39.**H.**
Cow. 26/7/39.**L.**
Cow. 22/3/41.**G.**
Cow. 8/5/43.**H.**
Cow. 30/7-28/8/45.**G.** *Screw rev.fitted.*
Cow. 13/9-9/10/46.**G.**
Cow. 8/12/48-18/1/49.**H/I.**
Cow. 3-28/10/50.**H/I.**
Cow. 25/2-29/3/52.**G.**
Cow. 24/6-6/8/55.**H/I.**
Cow. 16-18/8/55.**N/C.**
Cow. 6-22/9/55.**C/L.**
Cow. 21/9-13/10/56.**C/L.**
Cow. 4-30/11/57.**G.**
Cow. 25-27/12/57.**N/C.**
Inv. 17/12/60-27/1/61.**L/I.**
A.W.S.fitted.
Inv. 6/9-8/11/63.**G.**
Inv. 29/11/63.**N/C.**
Cow. 1-23/4/66.**C/L.**

BOILERS:
D1846 (C1445).
1430 *(ex1404)* 4/1/36.
1802 *(ex1413)* 22/3/41.
1442 *(ex1406)* 9/10/46.
27625 *(ex5905)* 29/3/52.
27619 *(ex65902)* 30/11/57.
27632 *(ex64711 &. spare)* 8/11/63.

SHEDS:
St Margarets.
Thornton Junction 29/12/62.
Dunfermline 7/1/63.

RENUMBERED:
5918 1/9/46.
65918 18/1/49.

CONDEMNED:
19/11/66.
Sold for scrap to Arnott Young, Old Kilpatrick.

1422

Darlington.

To traffic 19/3/26.

REPAIRS:
Dar. 20/10-1/12/31.**G.**
Cow. 8/9/34.**G.**
Cow. 21/3/36.**G.**
Cow. 27/4/36.**L.**
Cow. 13/9/37.**G.**
Cow. 24/2/40.**G.**
Cow. 16/5-6/6/42.**G.**
Cow. 26/10/43.**L.**

Cow. 13/5/44.**H.**
Cow. 7/6/44.**L.**
Cow. 21/7/44.**L.**
Cow. 9-23/6/45.**L.**
Cow. 8/11-6/12/45.**G.** *Screw rev.fitted.*
Cow. 15-29/6/46.**L.**
Cow. 12/12/47-27/2/48.**H/I.**
Cow. 27/3-15/4/50.**L/I.**
Cow. 4/3-5/4/52.**G.**
Cow. 5-27/3/54.**H/I.**
Cow. 10/12/54-1/2/55.**C/H.**
Dee. 9-20/9/55.**C/L.**
Cow. 16/8-8/9/56.**H/I.**
Cow. 9-28/1/59.**H/I.**
Cow. 7/11-16/12/60.**L/I.**
Cow. 21/8-16/9/61.**G.**

BOILERS:
D1847 (C1446).
1451 *(ex1428)* 8/9/34.
1460 *(ex1446)* 21/3/36.
1438 *(ex1401)* 13/9/37.
1447 *(ex1443)* 6/6/42.
27606 *(ex65933)* 5/4/52.
27579 *(ex65905)* 1/2/55.
27517 *(ex65913)* 16/9/61.

SHED:
St Margarets 24/3/26.

RENUMBERED:
5919 1/9/46.
65919 15/4/50.

CONDEMNED:
20/8/64.
Sold for scrap to Ardmore Steel, Craigendoran.

1423

Darlington.

To traffic 19/3/26.

REPAIRS:
Dar. 20/10-8/12/31.**G.**
Cow. 24/2/34.**G.**
Cow. 10/8/35.**G.**
Cow. 15/5/37.**H.**
Cow. 19/3/38.**G.**
Cow. 29/4/39.**G.**
Cow. 29/3/41.**G.**
Cow. 12/5/42.**H.**
Cow. 28/11/42.**H.**
Cow. 23/11/43.**L.**
Cow. 8/7/44.**G.**
Cow. 22/11/45-19/1/46.**L.**
Cow. 21/4-3/5/47.**H/I.** *Screw rev.fitted.*
Cow. 20/10/47-9/3/48.**H/I.**
Cow. 23/3-22/4/50.**G.**
Cow. 18/3-26/4/52.**H/I.**
Cow. 14/9-24/10/53.**H/I.**
Cow. 14/10-12/11/55.**G.**

Cow. 24/12/57-31/1/58.**G.**
Inv. 23/3-19/5/60.**H/I.**
A.W.S.fitted.
Inv. 19/7-2/9/60.**N/C.**
Inv. 14-23/3/61.**N/C.**
Inv. 28/5-6/6/62.**G.**
Inv. 12/5-7/8/65.**H/I.**

BOILERS:
D1849 (C1447).
1453 *(ex1437)* 24/2/34.
1431 *(ex1446)* 10/8/35.
1459 *(ex1445)* 19/3/38.
1453 *(ex1428)* 8/7/44.
1803 *(ex5908)* 22/4/50.
1803 Ren. 27500 26/4/52.
27495 *(ex64869)* 12/11/55.
27581 *(ex64815)* 31/1/58.
27655 *(ex65931)* 6/6/62.

SHEDS:
St Margarets 24/3/26.
Dalry Road 12/10/64.
Thornton Junction 7/3/65.

RENUMBERED:
5920 1/9/46.
65920 22/4/50.

CONDEMNED:
19/11/66.
Sold for scrap to Arnott Young, Old Kilpatrick.

1424

Darlington.

To traffic 25/3/26.

REPAIRS:
Dar. 5/5-20/6/32.**G.**
Cow. 10/2/34.**G.**
Cow. 7-28/12/35.**H.**
Cow. 3/9/37.**H.**
Cow. 13/5/39.**G.**
Cow. 4-18/5/40.**G.**
Inv. 17/7/42.**L.**
Cow. 28/11/42.**H.**
Cow. 11/2/44.**L.**
Cow. 9/8/44.**L.**
Cow. 12/4-3/5/45.**G.** *Screw rev.fitted.*
Cow. 4-19/10/46.**L/I.**
Cow. 5-28/5/49.**H/I.**
Cow. 28/8-14/10/50.**G.**
Cow. 16-20/2/51.**N/C.**
Cow. 28/1-20/2/54.**H/I.**
Cow. 4/10-10/11/56.**G.**
Cow. 28/7-29/8/58.**L/I.**
Inv. 3/3-5/5/60.**G.**
Cow. 18/8/61.**N/C.**
Inv. 8/3-12/4/63.**L/I.**
Cow. 7-30/1/65.**C/L.**
Cow. 28/6-9/7/66.**C/L.**

Thornton's 65901 was one equipped for carrying a snow plough, and when so fitted, the vacuum standpipe was temporarily removed. It was one on which the front buffers had been changed from double-case to Group Standard type, but it kept top lamp iron with G.N.R. pattern clover-leaf bracket fixing, never changing, as most did, to the Group Standard type. It had the electrification warning flashes put on boiler and cab for any work it had to do in the Glasgow district. *J.L.Stevenson*

As built, the top lamp iron followed North Eastern Railway custom in being mounted above the smokebox, and for access to it, two footsteps were fitted on the front plate. From 1935 Cowlairs gradually substituted a Group Standard iron mounted on the door, and most had that type before the end of the L N E R. 65929 had not been so changed when seen in October 1949, but 65920 here on 26th July 1953 at Seafield had "belt *and* braces". A 1958 photograph however showed that the smokebox top iron had been removed. *WBY collection*

Beginning with 65920 in May 1960, by February 1961 fourteen had been equipped with British Railways' Automatic Warning System, evidenced here on 65930 by the protection plate behind the front coupling, also the battery box in front of the cab, and the brake cylinder on the running plate. That A.W.S. facility was not then extended to the rest of the class. Note that the footsteps on the front of the smokebox have been removed, but only this one is known to have lost them. *J.L.Stevenson*

BOILERS:
D1850 (C1448).
  1440 *(ex1440)* 18/5/40.
  1432 *(ex1408)* 3/5/45.
  2025 *(new)* 14/10/50.
  2025 Ren. 27575 20/2/54.
  27617 *(ex65923)* 10/11/56.
  27707 *(ex64769)* 5/5/60.

SHEDS:
Thornton Junction 29/3/26.
Dunfermline 9/12/63.
Thornton Junction 21/11/65.

RENUMBERED:
 5921 14/9/46.
65921 28/5/49.

CONDEMNED:
19/11/66.
Sold for scrap to Arnott Young,
Old Kilpatrick.

1426

Darlington.

To traffic 26/3/26.

REPAIRS:
Dar. 3/3-24/4/31.**G.**
Cow. 11/33-7/12/33.**G.**
Cow. 6/10/34.**G.**
Cow. 11/7/36.**G.**

Cow. 13/8/36.**L.**
Cow. 1/12/38.**H.**
Cow. 21/6/41.**G.**
Cow. 19/1/43.**L.**
Cow. 31/7/43.**H.**
Cow. 4/9/43.**L.**
Cow. 12/8-7/9/45.**G.** *Screw*
rev.fitted.
Inv. 14/9-12/10/46.**L/I.**
Cow. 31/10-29/11/47.**H/I.**
Cow. 13/6-12/8/50.**G.**
Cow. 21-24/8/50.**N/C.**
Cow. 4-23/9/50.**C/L.**
Cow. 22/4-23/5/53.**H/I.**
Cow. 19/4-21/5/55.**G.**
Cow. 1/4-4/5/57.**H/I.**
Cow. 15-18/5/57.**N/C.**
Inv. 17/5-15/7/60.**G.**
Inv. 8-16/8/60.**N/C.** *A.W.S.fitted.*
Inv. 4/2-2/3/61.**N/C.**
Inv. 9/7-16/8/63.**H/I.**
Inv. 20-23/8/63.**N/C.**

BOILERS:
D1852 (C1449).
  1443 *(ex1419)* 7/12/33.
  1446 *(ex1422)* 6/10/34.
  1443 *(ex1405)* 11/7/36.
  1435 *(ex1414)* 21/6/41.
  1440 *(ex1424)* 7/9/45.
  2022 *(new)* 12/8/50.
  2022 Ren. 27572 23/5/53.
  27548 *(ex64941)* 21/5/55.
  27710 *(ex64709)* 15/7/60.

SHEDS:
Dundee 27/3/26.
Dunfermline 12/12/43.
St Margarets 10/11/54.
Thornton Junction 14/9/64.

RENUMBERED:
 5922 1/9/46.
65922 12/8/50.

CONDEMNED:
19/10/66.
Sold for scrap to Motherwell
Machinery & Scrap, Wishaw.

1427

Darlington.

To traffic 30/3/26.

REPAIRS:
Cow. 28/11/31-4/2/32. **G.** *Vac.*
brake removed.
Dar. 24/5-7/6/33.**L.** *New tender.*
Cow. 28/9/34.**G.**
Cow. 22/1/37.**G.**
Cow. 6/3/39.**H.**
Cow. 16/8/41.**H.**
Cow. 3/10/42.**L.**
Cow. 20/2/43.**G.**
Cow. 29/3/43.**L.**
Cow. 2/9/44.**H.**
Cow. 2-16/2/46.**L.**

Cow. 26/5-12/7/47.**G.** *Screw*
rev.fitted.
Cow. 9/7-7/8/48.**L/I.**
Cow. 23/1-11/2/50.**L/I.**
Cow. 19/8-6/9/52.**G.**
Cow. 25/10-13/11/54.**H/I.**
Cow. 10/7-18/8/56.**C/H.**
Thj. 9-17/12/57.**C/L.**
Cow. 26/2-22/3/58.**H/I.**
Cow. 29/8-22/9/61.**G.**
Cow. 31/7-6/8/62. *Not repaired.*
Cow. 6/8/62. *Put into store.*

BOILERS:
D1853 (C1450).
  1437 *(ex1400)* 22/1/37.
  1438 *(ex1422)* 20/2/43.
  1439 *(ex5900)* 12/7/47.
  27617 *(ex65912)* 6/9/52.
  27569 *(ex65910)* 18/8/56.
  27485 *(ex65903)* 22/9/61.

SHEDS:
Thornton Junction 1/4/26.
Dundee 5/6/28.
Aberdeen 1/1/33.
Dundee 30/9/34.
Dunfermline 12/12/43.

RENUMBERED:
 5923 24/11/46.
65923 7/8/48.

CONDEMNED:
29/12/62.
Cut-up at Cowlairs.

From new through to withdrawal all were in black, but until the June 1928 painting economies they did have single red lining. L N E R in 7½", and 12" figures in shaded transfers adorned their tenders, and in accordance with Darlington custom, all had CLASS J38 in white 2" high, painted on front buffer beam. *WBY collection*

Engines shopped by Cowlairs in 1929 to late 1931 had running number moved from tender to cab, but that works still used only 7½" L N E R on tender. They also discarded the red lining, and the classification on the buffer beam. *T.G.Hepburn*

From 1931 to their first tender repainting after July 1942, J38 standard 'livery' was unlined black but lettered and numbered as shown by 1442. *WBY collection*

In July 1942, Gresley's successor decided that there were savings of cost and labour to be made by simply showing N E on the tender. He also ordained that the word CLASS could be omitted on the buffer beam. *J.L.Stevenson*

The general renumbering of 1946 changed J38s into sequence from 5900 to 5934, and there was a slow return to L N E R in full on the tender, but not all had been fortunate to get it before nationalisation caused an increase of 60,000 to the running number. 5927 ex Cowlairs on 20th March 1948 is believed to be the last put into that style. *J.L.Stevenson*

Cowlairs only incurred the expense of a repainting after it had become really needed, and they ignored doing so simply to bring anything into a changed style. That threw up some distinctly odd pairings such as 65923 portrays. The numbering was a Cowlairs patching in August 1948, but the N E on the tender dated its last painting as done in February 1943. *J.Robertson*

65917 shows the first British Railways style used by Cowlairs. Note 12" size figures retained on the cab, also $4^{1}/_{2}$" on the buffer beam, but both without any shading, and using the wrong 6 and 9 figures for conforming to Gill Sans standard. Omitting CLASS allowed the name of the allocated shed (DUNFERMLINE in this case) to be shown. *J.L.Stevenson*

1428

Darlington.

To traffic 1/4/26.

REPAIRS:
Cow. 2-3/28.**G.**
Cow. 9/12/33.**L.**
Cow. 12/5-1/6/34.**G.**
Cow. 28/3-18/4/36.**G.**
Cow. 29/9/37.**L.**
Cow. 2/2/38.**H.**
Cow. 25/11/39.**H.**
Cow. 14/9/40.**L.**
Cow. 13-27/12/41.**G.**
Cow. 10/4/43.**L.**
Cow. 23/10-6/11/43.**G.**
Cow. 13/5-6/6/45.**H/I.**
Cow. 26/10-9/11/46.**L.**
Cow. 9/9-1/11/47.**G.** *Screw rev.fitted.*
Cow. 29/12/49-21/1/50.**H/I.**
Cow. 8/7-8/8/52.**G.**
Thj. 11-20/5/54.**C/L.**
Inv. 24/2-25/3/55.**L/I.**
Cow. 22-24/11/55.**N/C.**
Cow. 16-28/4/56.**N/C.**
Cow. 18/3-12/4/58.**G.**
Cow. 22-24/4/58.**N/C.**
Inv. 7/12/59-6/1/60.**L/I.**
Inv. 20/1/60.**N/C.**
Cow. 18/1-10/2/62.**H/I.**
Cow. 27-28/4/62.**C/L.**

BOILERS:
D1854 (C1451).
 1433 *(ex1407)* 1/6/34.
 1427 *(ex1400)* 18/4/36.
 1453 *(ex1406)* 27/12/41.
 1452 *(ex1447)* 6/11/43.
 27600 *(ex65911)* 8/8/52.
 27466 *(ex65913)* 12/4/58.

SHED:
Dunfermline 3/4/26.

RENUMBERED:
5924 7/11/46.
65924 21/1/50.

CONDEMNED:
29/6/64.
Sold for scrap to Motherwell Machinery & Scrap, Wishaw.

1434

Darlington.

To traffic 7/4/26.

REPAIRS:
Dar. 10/4-29/5/31.**G.**
Dar. 13/7-24/8/33.**G.**
Cow. 16/5/35.**G.**

Late in 1948 Cowlairs reduced the cab numbering to 10" so as to match the lettering on the tender, but still using the wrong style 6 and 9. In contrast, note that the 6 and 9 have been cast correctly on the plate fitted to the smokebox door. 65918 is as seen on 5th February 1949, and all plates checked had the correct Gill Sans figures, and not those with the surplus tail to them. Smokebox plate position was below the top hinge strap, but 65914 and 65932 had it above the strap. *J.L.Stevenson*

Cow. 23/1/37.**G.**
Cow. 7/2/39.**H.**
Cow. 23/1/41.**H.**
Cow. 21/2-21/3/42.**G.**
Cow. 2/7/43.**L.**
Cow. 23/9/44.**H.**
Cow. 4/4-1/6/46.**G.** *Screw rev.fitted.*
Cow. 4/4-10/5/47.**H/I.** *New cylinders.*
Cow. 4/7-4/8/49.**H/I.**
Cow. 3/4-3/5/52.**G.**
Cow. 22/5/52.**N/C.**
Cow. 1/11/52.**C/L.**
Cow. 19/2/53.**C/L.**
Thj. 22/1-1/2/54.**C/L.**
Cow. 20/4-14/5/55.**H/I.**
Cow. 25-28/5/55.**N/C.**
Cow. 29/10-30/11/57.**G.**
Cow. 28/4-17/5/58.**C/L.**
Inv. 23/2-31/3/60.**L/I.**
Cow. 19/11-8/12/62.**G.**
Inv. 2/7-18/9/65.**C/L.**
Inv. 14/10-20/11/65.**N/C.**

BOILERS:
D1855 (C1452).
 1439 *(ex1414)* 23/1/37.
 1427 *(ex1428)* 21/3/42.
 1431 *(ex1446)* 1/6/46.
 27604 *(ex65916)* 3/5/52.
 27591 *(ex64791)* 30/11/57.
 27824 *(ex65933)* 8/12/62.

SHEDS:
Dunfermline.
Thornton Junction 5/6/28.

RENUMBERED:
5925 1/9/46.
65925 4/8/49.

CONDEMNED:
21/11/66.
Sold for scrap to Arnott Young, Old Kilpatrick.

1437

Darlington.

To traffic 14/4/26.

REPAIRS:
Cow. 30/6/31.**L.** *Vac. brake removed.*
Dar. 16/12/31-4/2/32.**G.** *Vac. brake restored.*
Cow. 16-30/12/33.**G.**
Cow. 10/10/34.**H.**
Cow. 10/8/35.**G.**
Cow. 15/10/36.**H.**
Cow. 7/3/38.**G.**
Cow. 30/6/39.**L.**
Cow. 4/11/39.**G.**
Cow. 17/5/41.**G.**
Cow. 6/3/43.**H.**
Cow. 14/10/44.**G.**
Cow. 29/9-6/10/45.**L.**
Cow. 16/2-2/3/46.**L.**
Cow. 17/3-3/4/47.**H/I.** *Screw rev.fitted.*
Cow. 2/11-17/12/49.**G.**
Cow. 7/2-4/3/50.**H/I.**
Cow. 25/12/51-9/2/52.**H/I.**
Cow. 24/7-9/9/52.**C/L.**
Cow. 21/5-26/6/54.**G.**
Cow. 23/4-1/6/57.**H/I.**
Cow. 26/5-12/6/59.**G.**
Cow. 24-25/6/59.**N/C.**
Inv. 18/6-14/10/60.**C/L.**
A.W.S.fitted.

Inv. 14/7-5/9/62.**L/I.**
Inv. 1/7-9/8/63.**C/L.**

BOILERS:
D1857 (C1453).
 1449 *(ex1426)* 30/12/33.
 1432 *(ex1413)* 10/8/35.
 1460 *(ex1422)* 7/3/38.
 1429 *(ex1405)* 4/11/39.
 1803 *(ex1410)* 17/5/41.
 1449 *(ex1417)* 14/10/44.
 1456 *(ex5904)* 17/12/49.
 1456 Renumbered 27623 9/9/52.
 27605 *(ex65932)* 26/6/54.
 27430 *(ex62755)* 12/6/59.

SHED:
Dunfermline 19/4/26.

RENUMBERED:
5926 14/9/46.
65926 17/12/49.

CONDEMNED:
26/2/65.
Sold for scrap to Motherwell, Machinery & Scrap, Wishaw.

1440

Darlington.

To traffic 15/4/26.

REPAIRS:
Cow. 10/27.**G.**
Cow. 14/12/33.**G.**
Cow. 2/11/35.**G.**
Cow. 18/9/36.**L.**
Cow. 29/10/37.**H.**

When 65926 was ex works on 17th December 1949, the 10" tender lettering had been superseded by the B.R. emblem, and the status of J38 class was recognised by it being allowed the 28" size, other goods engines (including J37 class) only having 15½" emblem. Even after two years of British Railways ownership, Cowlairs paint shop were still putting tails on 6 and 9 cab figures. *J.L.Stevenson*

Cow. 4/11/39.**G.**
Cow. 15/6/40.**G.**
Cow. 19/9/42.**H.**
Cow. 30/10/43.**L.**
Cow. 21/10/44.**G.**
Cow. 29-14/9/46.**L.**
Cow. 21/12/46-14/6/47.**G.**
Cow. 26/2-13/3/48.**G.** *Screw rev.fitted.*
StM. 10/1-7/2/50.**C/L.**
Cow. 5/6-8/7/50.**L/I.**
Cow. 2/10-4/11/50.**C/H.**
Cow. 22/10-15/11/52.**H/I.**
Cow. 1/7-20/8/54.**L/I.**
Cow. 20/12/55-28/1/56.**G.**
Cow. 24/1-14/2/59.**L/I.**
Cow. 11/12/59-6/2/60.**G.**
Inv. 29/3-3/5/63.**L/I.**
Inv. 7-10/5/63.**N/C.**

BOILERS:
D1858 (C1454).
  1440 *(ex1415)* 2/11/35.
  1460 *(ex1437)* 4/11/39.
  1434 *(ex1408)* 15/6/40.
  1459 *(ex1423)* 21/10/44.
  1709 *(ex5906)* 14/6/47.
  2024 *(new)* 4/11/50.
  2024 Ren. 27574 15/11/52.
  27571 *(ex65934)* 28/1/56.
  27767 *(ex64854)* 6/2/60.

SHEDS:
St Margarets.
Dunfermline 14/9/64.

RENUMBERED:
  5927 14/9/46.
65927 8/7/50.

CONDEMNED:
30/12/64.
Sold for scrap to Shipbreaking Industries, Faslane.

1441

Darlington.

To traffic 15/4/26.

REPAIRS:
Cow. 12/3/33.**H.**
Cow. 5/10/35.**G.**
Cow. 17/3/37.**H.**
Cow. 19/3/38.**G.**
Cow. 30/6/39.**H.**
Cow. 12/8/39.**L.**
Cow. 9/11/40.**G.**
Cow. 8/11/41.**L.**
Cow. 5/9/42.**H.**
Cow. 20/11/43.**G.**
Cow. 4-25/5/45.**G.** *Screw rev.fitted.*
Cow. 6-13/10/45.**L.**
Cow. 7-14/12/46.**L.**
Cow. 14/12/47-23/1/48.**G.**
Cow. 9-25/3/50.**H/I.**
Cow. 2/2-7/3/53.**G.**
Cow. 9/9-2/10/54.**H/I.**
Cow. 8/5-8/6/57.**G.**
Inv. 7/3-13/4/60.**H/I.**
Cow. 27-28/2/61.**N/C.**
24/9/62. *Put into store.*

BOILERS:
D1859 (C1455).
  1453 *(ex1423)* 5/10/35.
  1461 *(ex1447)* 19/3/38.
  1450 *(ex1405)* 20/11/43.
  27743 *(ex64906)* 7/3/53.
  27624 *(ex65914)* 8/6/57.

SHEDS:
Dundee.
Dunfermline 12/12/43.

RENUMBERED:
  5928 14/9/46.
65928 25/3/50.

CONDEMNED:
29/12/62.
Cut-up at Inverurie.

1442

Darlington.

To traffic 15/4/26.

REPAIRS:
Cow. 6/28.**G.**
Dar. 19/1-26/2/32.**G.**
Cow. 19/9/34.**G.**
Cow. 18/4/36.**G.**
Cow. 21/10/36.**H.**
Cow. 9/9/39.**L.**
Cow. 11/11/39.**H.**
Cow. 22/6/40.**L.**
Cow. 27/12/41.**G.**
Cow. 14/7/42.**L.**
Cow. 12/12/42.**L.**
Cow. 21/8/43.**H.**
Cow. 7-28/7/45.**L.**
Cow. 11-27/12/46.**G.** *Screw rev.fitted.*
Cow. 30/6-24/7/48.**L/I.**
Cow. 26/10-24/11/49.**G.**
Cow. 8-10/5/51.**C/L.**
Cow. 10/11/52-17/1/53.**G.**
StM. 20/4-1/5/54.**C/L.**
Cow. 5/7-20/8/55.**H/I.**
Cow. 24-25/8/55.**N/C.**
Cow. 6-10/9/55.**N/C.**
Cow. 12-20/11/56.**C/L.**
Cow. 14/2-15/3/58.**G.**
Cow. 5/12/60-14/1/61.**L/I.**
A.W.S.fitted.
Cow. 5/9-19/10/63.**G.**

BOILERS:
D1860 (C1456).
  1436 *(ex1420)* 18/4/36.
  1433 *(ex1407)* 27/12/41.

CONDEMNED:
29/12/62.
Cut-up at Inverurie.

1446 *(ex5911)* 27/12/46.
27519 *(ex65906)* 17/1/53.
27487 *(ex64877)* 15/3/58.
25834 *(ex64813)* 19/10/63.

SHEDS:
St Margarets.
Dunfermline 4/4/65.

RENUMBERED:
  5929 12/4/46.
65929 24/7/48.

CONDEMNED:
22/4/67.
Sold for scrap to Motherwell Machinery & Scrap, Wishaw.

1443

Darlington.

To traffic 3/5/26.

REPAIRS:
Cow. 12/30-1/31.**G.**
Dar. 22/5-28/6/33.**G.**
Cow. 2/11/35.**G.**
Cow. 30/5-13/6/36.**G.**
Cow. 19/8/37.**L.**
Cow. 22/4/38.**H.**
Cow. 9/9/39.**L.**
Cow. 27/3-18/4/40.**G.**
Cow. 20/11/41.**L.**
Cow. 26/2-27/3/42.**G.**
Cow. 9/2-8/3/43.**L.**
Cow. 29/1/44.**H.**
Cow. 17/10-1/11/45.**G.** *Screw rev.fitted.*
Cow. 6/4-22/6/46.**L.**
Cow. 25/3-22/5/48.**G.**
Cow. 8-13/11/48.**C/L.**
Cow. 30/3-25/4/51.**L/I.**
Cow. 20/7-22/8/53.**G.**

Effective from mid-June 1957, the emblem was replaced by the crest from the grant of arms to British Railways, but for 18 months they boobed in applying it on the right hand side of tenders. The expensive transfers they bought showed the lion facing to the right, which was a serious mistake in heraldry. From Cowlairs in January 1958 from general repair, 65920 had one to which the College of Heralds objected. *Photomatic*

Cow. 5/10-5/11/55.**H/I.**
Dfu. 17-29/12/56.**C/L.**
Cow. 6/8-14/9/57.**G.**
Inv. 3/5-24/6/60.**L/I.** *A.W.S.fitted.*
Cow. 1-8/6/62.**N/C.**
Inv. 12/4-31/5/63.**G.**
Inv. 7-10/6/63.**N/C.**
Inv. 12/3-23/4/65.**C/L.**

BOILERS:
D1861 (C1457).
  1456 *(ex1444)* 2/1/35.
  1447 *(ex1407)* 13/6/36.
  1444 *(ex1444)* 27/3/42.
  1437 *(ex5917)* 22/5/48.
  1437 Ren. 27607 25/4/51.
  27492 *(ex64866)* 22/8/53.
  27467 *(ex64964)* 14/9/57.
  25833 *(ex64926)* 31/5/63.

SHEDS:
Stirling.
Dunfermline 6/12/26.
Thornton Junction 21/11/65.
Dunfermline 28/11/65.

RENUMBERED:
  5930 14/9/46.
65930 22/5/48.

CONDEMNED:
2/9/66.
Sold for scrap to Shipbreaking Industries, Faslane.

1444

Darlington.

To traffic 30/4/26.

REPAIRS:
Dar. 24/3-4/5/32.**G.**
Cow. 22/12/34.**H.**

Cow. 5/10/35.**G.**
Cow. 5/11/35.**L.**
Cow. 15/7/37.**H.**
Cow. 23/12/39.**H.**
Cow. 5/12/40.**L.**
Cow. 13/9-11/10/41.**G.**
Cow. 19/12/42.**H.**
Cow. 9/7/43.**L.**
Cow. 12/6/44.**L.**
Cow. 16-31/10/45.**G.** *Screw rev.fitted.*
Inv. 27/4/46.**L.**
Cow. 22-27/9/46.**L.**
Inv. 19/4-14/6/47.**G.**
Cow. 9-25/6/49.**H/I.**
Cow. 9/1-8/3/52.**G.**
Cow. 22/3-16/4/55.**L/I.**
Cow. 19-21/4/55.**N/C.**
Cow. 28/11/56-4/1/57.**G.**
Cow. 23/3-18/4/59.**L/I.**
Inv. 31/3-26/4/60.**N/C.**
Inv. 27/4-20/5/60.**N/C.**
Cow. 20/7-11/8/60.**N/C.**
A.W.S.fitted.
Inv. 10/7-1/9/61.**G.**
Inv. 6-28/2/64.**H/I.**

BOILERS:
D1862 (C1458).
  1441 *(ex1420)* 5/10/35.
  1429 *(ex1437)* 11/10/41.
  1451 *(ex1413)* 31/10/45.
  27610 *(ex5922)* 8/3/52.
  27655 *(ex64730)* 4/1/57.
  27500 *(ex64875)* 1/9/61.

SHEDS:
Stirling.
Dundee 3/12/26.
Thornton Junction 12/12/43.
Dunfermline 5/3/62.

RENUMBERED:
  5931 14/9/46.
65931 25/6/49.

CONDEMNED:
2/9/66.
Sold for scrap to Shipbreaking Industries, Faslane.

1445

Darlington.

To traffic 17/5/26.

REPAIRS:
Dar. 29/2-12/4/32.**G.**
Cow. 7/34.**H.**
Cow. 4/9/36.**L.**
Cow. 16/8/37.**G.**
Cow. 30/6/39.**H.**
Cow. 2/11/40.**G.**
Cow. 18/7/42.**H.**
Cow. 1/2/43.**L.**
Cow. 13/5/44.**G.**
Cow. 14-30/6/45.**L.**
Cow. 19/8-12/9/46.**H/I.** *Screw rev.fitted.*
Cow. 5/1-4/2/49.**G.**
Cow. 16/1-4/2/50.**C/H.**
Cow. 2-26/1/52.**L/I.**
Thj. 12-29/8/53.**C/L.**
Cow. 5/4-8/5/54.**G.**
Cow. 17/8-22/9/56.**H/I.**
Cow. 9-11/10/56.**N/C.**
Cow. 2-28/6/58.**G.**
Cow. 23/2-11/3/59.**C/L.**
Cow. 23/3-14/4/59.**C/H.**
Inv. 17/10-25/11/60.**L/I.**
Cow. 16/3-12/4/63.**L/I.**
Cow. 9-21/9/63.**C/L.**

BOILERS:
D1864 (C1459).
  1457 *(ex1404)* 16/8/37.
  1455 *(ex1420)* 2/11/40.
  1461 *(ex1441)* 13/5/44.
  1434 *(ex5907)* 4/2/49.

  1434 Ren. 27605 26/1/52.
  27614 *(ex65902)* 8/5/54.
  27600 *(ex65924)* 28/6/58.
  27435 *(ex62704)* 14/4/59.

SHEDS:
Dunfermline.
Thornton Junction 5/6/28.
Dunfermline 24/6/63.
Thornton Junction 9/12/63.

RENUMBERED:
  5932 24/3/46.
65932 4/2/49.

CONDEMNED:
3/3/66.
Sold for scrap to Geo.H.Campbell, Airdrie.

1446

Darlington.

To traffic 25/5/26.

REPAIRS:
Dar. 3/3-25/4/31.**G.**
Dar. 20/6-1/8/33.**G.**
Cow. 30/11/34.**G.**
Cow. 9/3-2/4/35.**G.**
Cow. 22/2/36.**G.**
Cow. 19/6/37.**H.**
Cow. 16/9/39.**H.**
Cow. 12/10/39.**L.**
Cow. 5-26/7/41.**G.**
Cow. 5/3/42.**L.**
Cow. 30/10/43.**H.**
Cow. 30/3/45.**L.**
Cow. 15/1-15/2/46.**G.** *Screw rev.fitted.*
Cow. 19/4/46.**H.**
Cow. 28/7-5/8/47.**L.**
Cow. 7/2-10/4/48.**L/I.**

By December 1958 action had been taken to make the crest acceptable and all J38 class except possibly 65902 were duly corrected. That one got the wrong crest in November 1957, and then to its withdrawal in December 1963 only had three light repairs. It would be a rare exception if Cowlairs included a repainting at any of them, but no photograph of 65902 in its final years has come my way - yet! Can **you** help? *R.F.Orpwood*

Cow. 15/1-10/2/51.**G.**
Cow. 3/5-4/6/52.**C/L.**
Cow. 3/2-6/3/54.**L/I.**
Cow. 29/2-21/4/56.**G.**
Cow. 19/5-14/6/58.**H/I.**
Cow. 26/9-4/10/58.**N/C.**
Inv.   23/6-25/8/60.**G. A.W.S.fitted.**
Inv.   13/1-3/3/61.**C/L.**
Cow. 11/6-13/7/62.**G.**

BOILERS:
D1865 (C1460).
  1431 *(ex1405)* 30/11/34.
  1460 *(ex1446)* 2/4/35.
  1445 *(ex1421)* 22/2/36.
  1431 *(ex1419)* 26/7/41.
  1435 *(ex1426)* 15/2/46.
  27582 *(new)* 10/2/51.
  27667 *(ex64879)* 21/4/56.
  27824 *(ex64829)* 25/8/60.
  27513 *(ex64815)* 13/7/62.

SHEDS:
Eastfield.
Dunfermline 5/6/28.

RENUMBERED:
  5933 7/4/46.
  65933 3/4/48.

CONDEMNED:
17/4/65.
Sold for scrap to Motherwell Machinery & Scrap, Wishaw

1447

Darlington.

To traffic 28/5/26.

REPAIRS:
Cow. 12/30-1/31.**G.**
Dar. 24/8-8/9/33.**G.**
Cow. 30/8/35.**G.**
Cow. 13/11-1/12/37.**G.**
Cow. 29/12/39.**H.**
Cow. 19/9-17/10/42.**G.**
Cow. 13/11/43.**H.**
Inv.   27/1-3/3/45.**L.**

Cow. 2-19/4/46.**G.** *Screw rev. fitted.*
Inv.   23/5/46.**L.**
Cow. 9/1-4/2/48.**H/I.**
Cow. 24/5-24/6/50.**G.**
Cow. 5/2/53.**N/C.**
Cow. 1/4-8/5/53.**H/I.**
Cow. 6/12/54-22/1/55.**C/L.**
Cow. 29/10-26/11/55.**G.**
Cow. 15/1-15/2/58.**H/I.**
Inv.   5/1-3/2/61.**G. A.W.S.fitted.**
Cow. 28/12/62-9/2/63.**G.**
Cow. 16-31/12/65.**C/L.**

BOILERS:
D1866 (C1461).
  1452 *(ex1434)* 1/12/37.
  1458 *(ex1404)* 17/10/42.
  1460 *(ex1411)* 19/4/46.
  2021 *(new)* 24/6/50.
  2021 Renumbered 27571 8/5/53.
  27589 *(ex64867)* 26/11/55.
  27510 *(ex64778)* 3/2/61.
  27588 *(ex65911)* 9/2/63.

SHEDS:
Eastfield.
Dunfermline 5/6/28.
St Margarets 10/11/54.
Thornton Junction 29/12/62.
Dunfermline 7/1/63.

RENUMBERED:
  5934 19/4/46.
  65934 24/6/50.

CONDEMNED:
31/12/66.
Sold for scrap to J.Mc William, Shettleston.

Here is the typical work on which J38 class spent a large part of their lives - taking coal away from its source to point of use. First the short haul on a colliery branch to the main line - as here at Monktonhall just south of Edinburgh - and then a trip to a power station, or even to serve shipping based on Aberdeen harbour. *J.J.Cunningham*

Being fitted with vacuum brake for engine and train made this class suitable for some passenger work. Here in 1928 at Inverkeithing Central Junction, 1447 is returning Glasgow holiday people on a summer Saturday from their stay at Fife coast resorts. *T.G.Hepburn*

All was not sunshine for this class. Thornton's 5931 and 5913 were derailed at Mawcarse when working a train to Perth in March 1947 due to a snow blizzard. The three men who look to be attempting to move 5913's tender must be incredible optimists. *W.Hennigan*

Approaching Joppa on 15th May 1948, no.5920 has a main line goods from Berwick to Edinburgh. Note that although ex Cowlairs from a heavy repair on 9th March 1948, its tender was lettered L N E R and not BRITISH RAILWAYS, nor did that works add any E prefix to the numbering. *J.J.Cunningham*

Their ability to handle passenger stock enabled J38 class to do filling-in work on station pilot duties, as Thornton's 65901 is doing here at Perth on 10th September 1962. It had worked there hauling a coal train, and was being employed to good use whilst awaiting its return trip on another train of empty wagons. *R.F.Orpwood*

Puissant to the very last, Thornton's 65911 as late as February 1967 has just crossed the river Forth at Alloa and is taking these empty coal hoppers from Perth back to the Fife coalfield. Maybe the leaking steam hastened its demise, which followed on 1st March 1967, leaving only 65901/29 in J38 class. *C.L.Kerr*

Another late example of J38 still hard at revenue earning was 65914 working alumina vans at Burntisland on 6th February 1965. Note this was one of the only two seen with smokebox numberplate *above* the door hinge strap. *J.L.Stevenson*

The occasional passenger train working by a J38 could still be seen in the mid-1950's and with no less than express headlamp indication, as carried by 65929 passing the Haymarket shed coaling tower. Those football supporters from Edinburgh would soon be crossing the Forth Bridge and were likely going to Kirkcaldy or Dundee. *WBY collection*

An almost indecent picture - certainly a sad one. 65913 on 12th September 1964 was being cut up at Cowlairs, where only 65923 also met its fate. Revealed are two details which could only be seen very rarely. The Spencer double-case buffers needed the beam to be drilled for the spindle to connect with the spring behind it, hence the holes. The front ring on a Diagram 97 boiler tapered to 6" longer at the bottom than at the top, and this view shows it clearly. That was why chimney and anti-vacuum valve were 6" further back when a J38 used a 97 boiler than on the original Diagram 97A.

WHICH ONE WOULD YOU CHOOSE?

Darlington's first effort at casting a fox for mounting above Hunt class nameplates displeased Gresley; it really does look too much like a shaggy dog. I am indeed fortunate to be able to show you how it compared with the second, and sleeker, animal with which we all became so familiar, but which can now only be seen with preserved nameplates. *WBY collection*